Life is too Serious to be Taken Seriously

Neville C. Goldrein C.B.E.

authorHOUSE®

AuthorHouse™ UK Ltd.
500 Avebury Boulevard
Central Milton Keynes, MK9 2BE
www.authorhouse.co.uk
Phone: 08001974150

First published by AuthorHouse 6/1/2010

ISBN: 978-1-4389-9498-7 (sc)

This book is printed on acid-free paper.

To Sonia

The light of my life

Prologue

From the moment of birth – although I do not recall the details – to the moment of death – and I have still to get there – life is a painful and generally a very serious experience. There are the problems from the start – how to walk, talk, learn, work, play, right through life. There are some lighter occasions but overall it is a pretty tough run, a very serious matter.

So one has two choices: Either to take it as it is, seriously, pondering over the problems, hoping for some lighter moments, but always struggling with all the difficulties which arise, or to look, and often one has to look hard, for the lighter side. Life is a very serious matter, but that is no reason to take it too seriously. One may as well enjoy the lighter sides to the full, make the best of the worst, and try to keep the smile going not only on one's face but, even more important, in one's mind. That is why I have always maintained that life is too serious to be taken seriously.

I was born in Hull, Yorkshire because my father's business, that of an egg importer, naturally required a port with easy access to Europe. I remember the 'horses and drays' – carts – bringing in loads of crates of eggs, which were unloaded and the eggs placed in large vats filled, I think, with lime, to preserve them. Then when eggs were required for sale they were literally fished out of the tanks with nets. They had to be checked, though, to see if any of them were bad, and so they were 'candled'. This was, I think, an invention of a cousin. It was rather like a beer can with a hole cut in the side and a candle inside it. Each egg was held up to the light of the candle and if there was any sign of a drop of blood or impurity it was thrown away.

My first school was Melfort House School, a small local kindergarten. I remember one day a knock at the front door of our house, and it was the schools inspector. I thought that he was going to drag me off there and then and I was terrified. My freedom was valuable to me even then. However he had come just to tell my mother that I had to start the following term. I must confess that even at that tender age – I was five, they started late in those days - it put me off because I never liked the idea of school, and these feelings stayed with me from the moment I went in to the moment I left. However even at that age there were some lighter moments. I was a new boy at school, and the teacher was a Mrs Bloomfield. I remember quite early on in my school days that she was going round the class looking at the work each of us had done, and in the course of this she leaned over the boy, or girl – I forget which, as one never noticed the difference at that age and in those days – and in so doing she presented her rather large posterior towards me. It was irresistible. I took my ruler and swiped her backside. 'Neville', she exclaimed, 'You naughty boy!'. I do not recall any punishment other than a ticking off, but had there been it would have been worth it. I remember that posterior to this day!

That dislike of school was not without good reason. First of all it deprived me of the liberty I had enjoyed up till the age of five. Indeed it was at about that time that I had my first personal brush with the law. I was playing in the 'back lane' behind our house, and 'fired' my potato pistol at another five-year-old whom I did not particularly like. I was a good shot then - I am now, although not with potatoes - and I hit him in the arm with the full force of the 'spat' of a small piece of wet potato - hardly lethal.

"I'll tell my mummy", he threatened, and discretion being the better part of valour I decided to make good my escape and go to the sanctuary of my own home. A few minutes later there was a knock at the front door, and behind the glass I could see the outline of a burly and helmeted policeman - and that was in the days when one respected, and indeed was terrified of, all policemen whether burly or not.

My mother answered the door. I hid in the shadows, with cold fear clutching at my heart at the prospect of immediate arrest or at least the cat. I heard something about a potato pistol and squeezed further into the corner.

"Neville", called my mother, "come here!". Here I went. The challenge was put to me of the heinous offence alleged against me. I instinctively exercised the two rights which I did not know I had, but which have assisted clients of mine, and me, for very many years - the safety of a denial and the right to silence.

I heard no more of it other than being told that I had been a naughty boy, but it may well be that this introduction to the law subconsciously indicated where my propensities lay. Fortunately they led me to the right side of the law.

I grew up in the sandwich era - the period in history when you did what your parents told you to do, and later on you did what your children told you to do. I could never win. The world has changed so much now. To my horror I find that I am talking historically.

However it did have certain advantages, perhaps more usually by good luck, but often because parental advice is not always rubbish - sometimes they are right. When I was quite young a cousin of mine married a solicitor. I, of course, knew nothing about solicitors or the law in those days and my parents, apart from buying a house and occasional business matters, knew little more. My father was in a business which did not involve much litigation - indeed at that time people were far less litigious than they are today - but he thought that the new cousin seemed to be very respectable and successful. So one day my parents told me and my brother, who was a few years older but in this respect probably no better informed, "You are going to be solicitors". In those days you did as you were told.

Whether it was insight, perspicacity, inspiration, or just good luck, I shall never know. The fact is that they chose the Law for me, and I enjoyed every moment of my association with it from the day I went up to Cambridge to the day of my retirement and continuing.

--oOo--

Chapter 1
The Great Unknown

Hymers College in Hull was a beautiful school – if you like schools. It was as good a day public school as you could hope to find. It had everything, and in its day was the state of the art. I have visited it recently too, and it is still state of the art. It had then forty acres of playing fields – it now has forty-five - and yet was only about a mile from the City centre. It was built on the site of the old Botanic Gardens. There were several rugger pitches, the First Eleven cricket pitch was kept specifically for the first eleven, and outside 'match time' no one walked on it other than the groundsman.

There was a complete cinder track, squash courts, tennis courts, woods, a lake – it was all there. As schools go, for facilities and education, one could not ask for better, but if school is not your favourite pastime then it was unsatisfactory from the start. I loved the School itself but I hated the whole idea of school. It would have been different if the masters had said, for example, 'Goldrein, would you be good enough to do some maths homework?'

Had they asked me like that it would have been difficult to object. But they gave orders! I think that was one of the reasons I enjoyed my higher education so much – it was up to me as to whether or not I worked, and so I was prepared to do it.

During World War II we were evacuated. What was an evacuee? We were schoolchildren moved from our homes in the cities to safer havens some distance away - evacuated. At the outbreak of World War II my school was evacuated to Pocklington, some miles from Hull. Evacuation was no fun: My first 'digs' were quite appalling, with three of us in the bed, a number of fleas, and no electric light allowed after 9 p.m.. I managed shortly afterward to move to better digs, where my 'foster mother' was a lovely lady, and her sister was kindness itself, and her husband one of the most unkind and awkward men I have ever met. For example, the meat ration might have been one chop per week. One week he disdainfully gave his to the dog, saying that she had cooked it badly, and then he took hers. He was an unqualified chemist, but one thing in his favour was that I liked photography, and he allowed me to process customers' films. Even when I ruined some during my 'training' he was gentle with me. The downside was that he often got so drunk as to have set his bed alight one night by going to sleep with a cigarette in his mouth. Added to that the household had to pass through my bedroom to get to the bathroom – and I mean bathroom, fortunately that did not include the loo – but that was hardly conducive to privacy.

We had our lessons in various church halls in the mornings, and in Pocklington Grammar School in the afternoons. We were pretty bomb-free but it was horrifying to hear the German night bombers flying overhead towards Hull, to hear the thump and thud of the bombs and to see my home town on fire from a distance of some twenty or so miles. And to telephone home was virtually impossible. Even in normal times there was no direct dialling for such a distance as twenty miles or so - all calls had to be made through the operator. Besides that the calls were expensive, and one could not really ask to use the telephone - if they had one - and so far as I recall there was no telephone in my digs.

I managed to get home for week-ends on the pretext that I needed treatment for my flat feet. They came in very handy later on in my career too! I was able to join my father at home - my mother was evacuated down south to avoid the 'blitz' - and we could be together. At night there was usually an air-raid. My father and I got so tired of running to the cold air-raid shelter in the garden and we usually stayed in bed with our heads under the covers and hoped that the bombs would miss. All the windows were taped to save glass flying in the event of bomb blasts, and if there had been a direct hit the shelter would not have saved us anyway. My poor father, and I adored him, was terrified by the noise of the bombs and anti-aircraft fire which was indeed very frightening but together we coped. Later on, when it got too bad, my father came to Pocklington each night and I at least saw him each evening, although he had a twenty mile or so commute to and from Hull each morning and evening, and in those says, and in wartime, that was quite a journey. He travelled by 'bus of course - there was no petrol for cars. Like most people then, though, we had no car anyway.

Anyway after over a year of this the family was going to move down south and I was to move to another school – Berkhampstead School. It was my last Friday at Hymers College. I was not too polite with the Latin master. "You will go to see the Headmaster after school", he told me. Untroubled, knowing there was nothing to fear as I would not be there, I readily agreed, and made no plea in mitigation.

After the last period my joy was unbounded. I ignored school rules. When one of the masters said "Put your cap on Goldrein", I replied gleefully, "I have left the school". I did not even call him 'sir' and went happily to my digs to pack up to move. Imagine my horror to find a telegram awaiting me to say that all arrangements were changed and that I was not moving to another school after all.

The following Monday morning I was back in the class-room. The first period was Latin. I sat in the front row. The master, who was fortunately for me extremely short-sighted, and I mean short-sighted, asked, "Where is the boy I sent to see the Headmaster on Friday?". A good friend of mine, Mike Lord, was sitting next to me in a double desk, in the front row. He saved me by saying, loud and clear, "That was Goldrein, sir, and he's left the school". I heard no more about it.

Anyway to come back to Pocklington; with the War, planning was difficult. It was difficult enough to organise things at the best of times but a divided family made things so much worse. I had taken my Higher School Certificate exams - the then equivalent of "A" Levels - and nobody had any great hope of success, with the result that there was no contingency plan to cover the unlikely event of my achieving a respectable pass. Still, I had some excuse because I was only 16 at the time.

Whether it was that they were bowled over with delight, or just suffering unbelieving shock and horror at the examination system, I do not know, but the family had no little difficulty in reconciling themselves to the impossible. I had not only passed, but passed well with a Distinction in English. I was the only one to get a Distinction as they were quite rare in those days. The only comment from our Sixth Form English master, who himself was an examiner for the Higher School Certificate of another Board, was "Goldrein, if you can get a Distinction then my standards must be wrong. I shall resign as an examiner".

I had been expected to stay another year at school to take the exams again - to get a better result than the one they expected me to get. There would have been plenty of time to make arrangements for University. Now there was no time, the family was temporarily split, and communications were poor, even by the standards of those days, because of the War.

It was decided that I should go up to Pembroke College Cambridge as soon as possible. The question was, how soon was soon?

--oOo--

Chapter 2

There was tremendous excitement at the thought of going up to Cambridge for many reasons. It was associated with winning Boat Races, the glamour of undergraduate pranks, the snobbery - it was after all one of the two greatest universities in the Country. (We used to think the only two, and there were very few universities then anyway). But above all it was to be the escape from evacuation and from something which I had loathed from the first second it started until the very moment I left - school.

To the extent that I had disliked school as an experience which I would have been delighted to avoid, Cambridge fulfilled its promise and offered me all I could have hoped for. I think I can fairly say that the time I spent there was the happiest I had known and I still look back on it with such fond memories.

One could ask, 'what was so wonderful about it?' Well, I had always been prepared to do things, get on with work, face the odd hardship, provided that I had it all explained to me or that I could ascertain the details, and that I respected the authority which imposed the rules. In addition, and this was important, I particularly preferred to be asked for co-operation rather than being compelled blindly to obey orders and instructions. At Cambridge I had the liberty to work or not to work. There was no compulsion. The surroundings were delightful, the company excellent, the stimulus to the grey matter was boundless, and the opportunities for revelry unending.

I was just seventeen when I went up, and because of the War one could, if one could manage it, and doing an extra term during the Long Vacation, get an honours degree in two years. I decided to have a bash at it rather than finish half a course, go into the army, and, if I survived, return to Cambridge to take my degree. I felt that life did not have enough time to spare for such luxuries.

On the other hand it seemed a terrible waste of Cambridge to work when there were so many other things to do. So I came to an arrangement with myself: I would enjoy Cambridge to the full whilst I was there, and work hard during the vacations, which were fairly long.

This may seem on the face of it to have involved quite a sacrifice, but in fact my family had just moved from Hull to Liverpool - my Father's business demanded a port, and with the War and German submarines in the North Sea threatening all shipping, Hull had to all intents and purposes ceased to be one. We were in a rented furnished house, I knew nobody, had no friends, and to work was really no great problem. It imposed, though, a self-discipline which I have found useful ever since.

Cambridge never had any really dull moments, but even there the academic life of lectures and supervisions (as we called tutorials) had to fit in with my personal scheme of things. One of our lecturers was a Mr Glanville Williams - when my son in due course went up to Cambridge many years later the same man was his Professor of Law. He gave his lectures - you could take your choice - on a Tuesday at 9 o'clock or Thursday at 11. I rejected Tuesday as 9 o'clock was far too early to get up. Gradually all the other undergraduates attended the Tuesday one and Glanville Williams asked me if I could, perhaps, do the same. I explained, "I am sorry, sir, but other commitments make that completely impossible". He did not ask the reason why. In the event I had my commitment – a lie-in – on a Tuesday, and a personal lecture on the Thursday.

We could, in the College Buttery, which was rather like our private grocery and wine store, buy a bottle of vintage port for five shillings, and so, of course, at the age of 17, I had to become a wine connoisseur. I formed a club which I called the "9 Club", being the 'One-Over-The-Eight Club', so that we could foster our youthful palates. We had a tie specially made with a light blue '9' on a dark blue bottle on a light blue tie.

I played squash, rowed - I was rather lightweight so I coxed badly instead of rowing badly - debated, and went to societies representing every different nationality, interest and viewpoint, including the Cambridge University Socialist Club. The S.T.C. - the Senior Training Corps – was the successor to the Junior Training Corps at school, to prepare one for the army. I was in the artillery and had my first meeting with reasonably heavy weapons. The title of the Corps – which pre-War had been known as the Officers' Training Corps - is interesting as at that time there was the assumption that every Cambridge graduate would, almost as of right, become a commissioned officer. Later, when I was in the army, I found that it was not quite as easy as that.

In those days undergraduates were obliged to wear 'academic dress' – a gown for lectures and for dining in Hall and a cap, or mortar board, with the gown when outside college after dark, It became a point of honour to have one's gown as scruffy as possible, so long as it remained a gown, and ones 'square', which was what we called a mortar board, had to be similarly scruffy. Some took out the wood from their squares, so that they flopped down like an old cleric's hat. I broke the wood in mine into four quarters, so that I could fold it up and put it in my pocket when I was indoors. When I opened it up I think I looked more like the Mikardo.

If you failed to wear academic dress after dusk you were liable to be 'progged'. There was the Proctor, a University don wearing full academic dress, who patrolled the streets accompanied by two 'bulldogs', college porters. They were dressed in dark suits with tails and top hats. One carried the Bible, and in theory any undergraduate was entitled to ask the Proctor to read the lesson for the day.

One evening I was in Trumpington Street and fairly near to Pembroke, not wearing a cap, when I saw the Proctor approach. I jumped on to the steps of Corpus Christi College as the steps of any college were sanctuary. However after half an hour, and the Proctor and his team did not move, I realised I had to be caught. We had to be in College by midnight and time was getting short. So I stepped down. One of the bulldogs came up to me, raised his top hat, and asked, "Are you a gentleman of this University sir?". "Yes", I replied. "Will you kindly have a word with the Proctor sir?". "Yes", I replied again. The Proctor came up, raised his square, and asked "Are you a gentleman of this University sir?". I felt I had been here before. "Yes sir", I replied. "Your name sir?", he asked. "Goldrein, sir". "Your college sir?", he asked. "Pembroke, sir", I replied. "You will be fined six shillings and eightpence sir", he said. "Certainly sir". "Goodnight sir". "Goodnight sir". I should mention that the fine was the equivalent of 33p, and about £10 or more at today's prices. Six shillings and eightpence was the old English mark. In those days, and indeed for some years after, solicitors, including me, used to charge six and eightpence for advice.

It was not just a question of 'academic dress'. We had to wear a jacket and tie for lectures and in hall, apart from a gown. The usual dress was a college blazer, a college scarf - each college had its own - and corduroy trousers. The thought of the present-day jeans and anorak with sneakers still leaves me dazed.

Another rule was to be in College, your own College, by 10pm. If you came in after ten but before 11 there was a 'gate fine' to be paid. Up to midnight there was a bigger gate fine. After midnight the gate was locked. That could result in a fine or rustication – being sent home for the rest of the term.

This being so there were two incentives to get in after midnight. One was that one may have been out and midnight was too early. The other was the challenge of another rule to break. So we used to climb into college hoping that we would not be caught. I arranged one evening with a friend that there would be a thread of strong black cotton hanging from his upstairs window which would not be seen in the dark. One must remember that there was a very strict blackout. There were no street lights in case they guided enemy bombers, and even car headlights were reduced to a narrow strip. In fact there were few cars in those days, and during the War even fewer because of the shortage of petrol.

I pulled the black cotton, as arranged, and down came a rope attached to it. I put my weight on the rope when I heard a great banging and crashing from upstairs, the sound of moving furniture, and I realised that the rope was attached to his bed. As soon as I put my weight on it I awoke my friend by dragging him, bed and all, across the room until the bed reached the window.

Then I started to climb. I was just about there twice when, each time, a car came past, and even with his headlights partly blacked out in case of air raids, I was still illuminated and dropped quickly to ground, trying to look casual although my gown was flowing and my square was tipped over one eye. The third time I managed to get to the top but realised that the window sill was large being about a foot from base to the window and at a diagonal. It was nearly impossible to stretch a hand over this length of stone. Ultimately with a hand up by my friend I got in. But it was worth it! I had beaten the system.

There was some sense in these rules though, like the rule that you could not 'sport the oak', or in other words close the oak front door to your set - your rooms - if there was a woman there. It was not the ideal contraceptive but it must have helped, as the penalty for a breach of the rule was to be 'sent down' - expelled.

Times have changed a lot. I was at Pembroke College not long ago with my wife. We stayed in one of the guest rooms. Imagine my shock when I went up to my old set consisting of a bedroom and a sitting room, to find that it had been split in to two bed-sitters. One room was occupied by a man and the other by a woman - and that was official. The 'oak', which was still the main outside door, was outside both rooms.

I did indeed, as I had promised myself, work during the vacations, within reason, and to my enormous surprise and relief, and the end of my second year, I found that I was a B.A. and had achieved a good Honours degree. I was still eighteen.

--oOo--

Chapter 3

Having had my call-up deferred for about six months to enable me to get my degree the Army wasted little time in pulling me in. I was told to report to Carlisle, to a Primary Training Wing. I was told to take basic personal items, but the army was to provide most of what was needed.

I tried to think of the worst possible scenario, so that I would not be disappointed by what I found. I thought we would have to sleep, for example, in hospital-type beds, with coarse sheets, and probably as many as four or six in a room. The reality was rather different. We had to sleep on double-tier bunks, solid wood, with 32 men in one Nissen hut. A Nissen Hut was made out of corrugated iron sheets at the sides and curving up from the ground, with straight ends. That is where the door was and the few windows. There were no straight walls apart from the ends and corrugated iron is cold. Apart from that, when the sergeant wanted to awaken us in the morning he ran his stick along the corrugations outside making a noise rather like a machine gun. It woke us up with a start the first time. After that we were so tired and so used to it that we hardly heard it – but we still had to get up.

There was no heating other than a small iron stove in the middle for which, with wartime restrictions and fuel rationing, there was very little fuel, and we slept on straw palliasses or sleeping bags. We were given the bag part of the palliasse, and taken to a large shed full of straw, and told to fill our bags on which we were to sleep. I thought it was better to put in as much straw in as possible because it would flatten in time and I did not know if further supplies would become available. It was rather like eating a lot because you did not know where the next meal would come from. I did this, little realising that when I went to 'bed' I would be lying virtually on a fairly solid sausage, which was not only nearly as hard as a rock, but it was just about impossible to sleep on it. I was on the top bunk and kept rolling off the sausage.

I had taken with me, with my 'basic items' although the instruction did not list them, a pair of pyjamas to use until I got my army issue. Little did I realise that there was no 'pyjama issue' and that the custom was to sleep in your underwear, which was changed, after being worn day and night, once a week. I put the pyjamas in at the last moment, and without thinking it through, they happened to be green, pure silk, decorated with embroidery rather like a hussar's jacket. They had been given to me as a present some time before. They should have caused me two problems, but there was in fact only one. The first was that wearing silk pyjamas on a straw palliasse was rather like the princess sleeping on the pea. Every piece of straw could be felt through that lovely soft light material.

The other problem which could have arisen from my taking with me this particular pair of pyjamas (I had more normal ones at home which I could have used) was that I should have realised that the 'mickey' would have been taken out of me by the thirty-one others in the hut. However one of them, Arthur Prestt, who had read Law with me at Cambridge and who later in his career became Recorder of Manchester, wore pyjamas as well - the only other one to do so, although his were normal winceyette. I walked the length of the barrack room to speak to Arthur, thinking nothing of my pyjamas. But no mickey was taken, I think because I wore them so unselfconsciously that they were accepted. Again, at that time there was a positive 'class' distinction, and my 'class', deriving from public school and Cambridge, was, I suppose, entitled to wear silk green pyjamas. How the world has changed!

One thing we were issued with, though, sounded most attractive and unexpected. We were told that each of us would be issued with a housewife. I really felt that this was the ultimate in army welfare for the troops and looked forward in eager anticipation to the issue of this most important item. The great moment came! But to our disappointment the housewife consisted of a bundle containing needles, cotton, pins - a sewing kit. I always felt that a housewife was rather more than that. And fancy calling a sewing kit a housewife. You could hardly be more male chauvinistic than that. Nevertheless 'she' came in useful because I had to darn my own socks. When I say 'darn' I did not really go as far as that. I gathered the edges of the hole in the sock together and stitched them up. My feet got used to the blisters which followed.

We were all in the same boat, whatever our walk of life, and we all decided instinctively to make the best of it. Sleeping underneath me in our double hard wooden bunk was a great chap – he had done time but between him and me there was great trust. When I could not undo my locker he opened it for me in a flash. I could reciprocate because he was illiterate and I was able to write his letters home and read the replies to him. He seemed to feel no embarrassment and so I did not either, although the letters were often extremely personal – in the nicest possible way.

It was hard going, washing and shaving in cold water, one shower a week, and one change of underwear and socks a week. That was the army issue of underwear. In the summer we must have smelt to high heaven. Those in the army today do not know that they are alive! We ate out of mess tins - literally small tins with a handle. You queued up, food was sloshed in, and that was it. There was a choice - take it or leave it. Washing up was really a matter of chance. We had to use our mess tins for shaving water as well. The bristles probably made the dried egg taste better!

The A.T.S. girls – Auxiliary Territorial Service – were in those days the women's section of the army and they sloshed out the food, and sloshed out foul language as I had never heard from women before and was horrified.

Route marches of twenty miles were the norm - we stopped for ten minutes each hour for a rest or to relieve ourselves. If you needed to stop before the hour was up that was out of the question, whatever the urgency - or desperation. The facilities for the latter were, of course, nil, but we each had a small spade to dig slit trenches or to dig a hole for use as a temporary toilet. Privacy was, of course, non-existent.

One day we were on parade outside the main hall, where any lectures, and very occasional social occasions, took place. The sergeant called out – or I should say he shouted, (sergeants never 'called'.) - "Anyone 'ere with School Certificate?" (the equivalent of GCSEs). One or two, rather pleased with themselves, stepped forward. "Anyone 'ere with Higher School Certificate?". This brought forth another. Then "Anyone 'ere with a university degree?". That was my great moment. Clearly there was something to be gained from an education after all. Forward I stepped. The sergeant continued, "Right, you clever buggers, move the piano in there to the other hut - and you ignorant buggers, you watch how the clever ones do it". I learned one important lesson from that - in the army you never, but never, volunteer.

One day our platoon commander – there were about thirty-two men in a platoon and he was our officer - gave an order 'You're going to Brough'. Brough was the rifle range. It is strange that times have changed so much, but this officer spoke with a northern accent and even those with similar accents did not respect him as they would have respected a 'well-spoken' officer. I explained that I was playing rugger for the Company that afternoon, on the orders of the Major, the Company commander and this lieutenant's superior. He said again 'You're going to Brough'. I respectfully suggested that he should check. He did. I played rugger.

The torture seemed to go on forever, but it was only six weeks. There is no doubt that at the end of it we were tougher and more prepared and able to rough it than we had ever been in our lives.

The next move was for field training in Wales. I had asked to be posted to the Royal Artillery and the unit was stationed in Newtown. Here we were again in Nissen huts, and were awakened each morning in the same way as before by the sergeant running a piece of wood along the corrugated walls of the hut. After the 'machine-gunning' he would open the door, let in the freezing wind, and shout, "Leave your cock and grab a sock", and with those gentle and refined words of encouragement we got up. Having washed and shaved - in winter that literally meant breaking the ice - we had to leave our bunks in pristine condition before breakfast. If it were not properly laid out to within the regulation half inch you were in trouble. Sometimes the sergeant would kick it all aside about two minutes before we were due on parade, leaving you little time to make up your bed again – and it had to be perfect this time.

At our primary training wing we had used rifles. Here we fired field guns and it was a much more exhilarating experience. The other benefit, and one of the reasons I had wanted to be posted to the 'Gunners', as the Royal Artillery was known, was that field guns have to be towed by vehicles, and as the guns required men to work them they had to take us with in the vehicles and so there was no need to walk. I had one friend who went one better by joining the searchlights wing of the Royal Artillery. He preferred that because they 'didn't go bang'.

We were a long way away from home. From Newtown to my home, then in Liverpool would, today, take not more than an hour to an hour and a half. Then, with a wartime train service, no main lines and depleted services it took well over half a day. It would have made even present-day railway services seem like Utopia. A week-end leave, and we only had one, involved half of the time travelling. And of course there was no heating, and certainly no buffet car.

The next rung on the ladder, and it was a ladder that seemed to get longer and longer, was W.O.S.B., The War Office Selection Board, familiarly known as Wosbee. This was where they sent 'potential officers', and in those days you were considered to be a potential officer if you had been to University, or even if you had the then equivalent of 'A' Levels, provided, of course, that you had been to the 'right' sort of school. Looking back the curious thing is that these 'class privileges' did not seem to be resented by anyone. I fortunately had the requisite privileges, and I was unashamedly pleased to make the best of them. Such privilege seems to us today to be astonishing.

At Wosbee we spent the four days living in the same building and sharing the same 'mess' with the training officers. Our every move was supervised. We ate with the examining officers, an army psychiatrist, the colonel in command, and all those who not only assessed us in training but assessed our behaviour when relaxed. After all an officer would have to know how to behave himself in the Officers' Mess. Skills of leadership, strength of character, and all that were all very well but, perhaps even more important, you had to know how to hold a knife and fork. The only place where we were not under observation was - I hoped - the loo.

We had tests, interviews, had to make speeches on prepared and on-the-spot subjects and had to undergo medical examinations. There were practical tests too. One was that we were given some bits of wood, a rope, a few planks, and a box of 'valuable instruments'. There was a small stream and we had to build some kind of bridge to get the box to the other side. The assessing officers were watching our every move.

There were about a dozen of us. Three groups formed themselves, each with a different idea. I had no ideas at all and saw failure staring me in the face and my chance of being an officer disappearing for ever. Then I had a flash of inspiration. I looked at the three ideas the others were trying out and shouted to two of the three groups, "Stop what you're doing. Do it this way!", pointing to one of the three teams. In the army one had got used to 'jumping to it' when an order was given. They all did. I shouted more orders. They obeyed!

The bridge was finished, and I shouted "Carry the box of instruments to the other side". Half way over everything collapsed into the water

- including the potential officers. I got the credit for having shown 'qualities of leadership'!

We were, one by one, called in to the colonel and told our fate. He was a 'Gunner' and saw the Royal Artillery flashes on my shoulders. To him it was the 'Royal Regiment of Artillery, Right of the Line and Pride of the British Army'. He told me to sit down - a rare privilege. "Goldrein", he said, "you have passed". He went on, "But there is one problem". What could that be, if I had passed, I wondered. "The Country needs infantry officers but I am sure you would prefer to remain in the ranks of the Royal Regiment of Artillery". I thought, after all that hard work, that I was back to the beginning! Thinking of beds as opposed to bunks, a batman to clean my boots and tidy my belongings, eating off plates and not out of mess tins, wearing a smart service dress with Sam Browne belt instead of a rough serge battledress, far better toilet arrangements, hot water to wash in, no more barrack rooms, but primarily of course thinking of the interests of the King and Country, I said that I would prefer to have the opportunity to be an infantry officer. In disgust he told me that I would be posted to an infantry Officer Cadet Training Unit - OCTU - after a seven day leave.

Before going to OCTU we were posted to a place called Marsk, near Redcar in Yorkshire. There was very little for us to do as we awaited a posting, so I and two friends, Charlie Creed who was a world-renowned couturier from London and Paris, and 'Bonchy' Cohen, who owned a factory in Glasgow making battle-dresses got a room in Marsk to which we retired in the evenings to relax and chat. Charlie was completely bilingual French/English, and one evening when the landlady popped in to see how we were, he spoke to her in French saying the most dreadful things, with a smile. She thought he was complimenting her, thanked him, and then left us to our own devices.. Charlie's battle-dress was tailor-made in Savile Row and Bonchy's was specially made in his factory. I was the scruffy one.

--oOo--

Chapter 4
The Officer Cadet

J ust before I went into the army, the procedure was six weeks primary training and then to OCTU. By the time I finished primary training we had to have the field training at Newtown as well followed by OCTU. By the time I finished at Newtown you had to go to Pre-OCTU before going to OCTU proper. The nearer I thought I was getting to the officer stage the more I found that there was yet a further hurdle to cross. That badge of commissioned rank, which I hoped one day to wear on my shoulder, and the privileges which went with it, were fast becoming a mirage.

Pre-OCTU gave us the privilege of wearing small while flashes on our shoulders and on our forage caps, which at least gave us a little status. Living conditions were no better, and the training was far tougher than anything we had experienced before. One trial I remember particularly was my first 'ten miles in two hours' march. We had full kit, full water bottles, tin hats, rifles, full ammunition pouches, and ran for five minutes, marched for five minutes and then rested for two. It was hot weather by this time, and at one stage, towards the end, I passed out whilst I was running. The officer cadets on either side of me held me up until the next walking period. I came to as we slowed down, and I am still grateful for those two as, had I collapsed and anyone had noticed, I would have been returned to my unit, in the ranks and not as an officer, doubtless to the Royal Artillery, and fulfilled the colonel's desires.

Wrotham, where the pre-OCTU was situated in sunny scenic Kent, had, and doubtless still has, an escarpment. An escarpment is the nearest thing to a cliff without actually being one. I felt sure that the camp was not situated there for its natural beauty.

Whatever our training on any day those in charge always managed to ensure that we ended up at the bottom of the escarpment and then we had to climb up that escarpment to get back to the camp. It got higher and steeper every day. The sergeant instructors were there to turn us into officers, which meant, of course, training us to be their commanders. I cannot blame them for putting us through it, to the extent that the sergeant would say 'You're an 'orrible cadet, Goldrein, what are you?'. And my reply had to be, needless to say, 'A horrible cadet, sergeant'.

The course was six weeks of more unadulterated hell but as I was to find ultimately, you can even get used to hell. I was receiving, after all, a good ration of it. We lived in tents and 'facilities' were, to say the least, primitive. Nothing 'ensuite' there! I had foolishly concluded that nothing could be worse than that which I had endured before. How stupid of me! Even the locals were not very friendly, regarding us, I think, as the 'brutal soldiery', although at the end of a day's or a week's training we were far too exhausted to be brutal.

We went from there to OCTU at Barmouth in North Wales, and it was not by accident that it was surrounded by mountains - where it was not bounded by the sea. I had thought that the escarpment was steep........

--oOo--

- 26 -

We lived in better conditions - three to a room in a seafront hotel of about a one star quality - and ate in the 'officer cadets' mess' off plates - just imagine that - and using cutlery. That was luxury. We were waited on when we ate. We had a shared batman - a soldier whose duties were to look after us, keep our room tidy, clean our boots, press our uniforms, clean our kit and make our beds. He started to polish our smart Sam Browne belts right from the start so that when - or if - we got our commissions our leather would look well-worn. Indeed we had to go to the tailor to order our uniforms at the beginning to have them ready for when we passed out as officers. The tailors agreed that there would be no charge if we failed the course.

But once outside and in training it was a different story. The parade ground was on the edge of the sea. Mr Regimental Sergeant Major Cop of the Coldstream Guards made our previous mentors seem like kind nannies. He would march us towards the sea. He would 'forget' to shout the order to left or right wheel and let us continue until we were in the sea up to our ankles - making sure that the water was above boot level. He then ordered 'right wheel' which meant that everyone turned right and marched with water up to his ankles before he shouted 'right wheel' again to bring us back to dry land.

That may not sound too bad, but in winter and with soaking feet you carried on the day's training whatever the discomfort, and if your ruined boots were not in pristine condition the next morning you were on a charge.

I remember being on parade when it started to rain which, of course fell onto our bayonets as well as onto us. The bayonets were the big flat ones where we were taught to 'stick them in and then turn them before pulling them out'. That was to make absolutely sure that the recipient was dead. The raindrops, not unnaturally, marked the bayonets with little spots when the rain dried off. "Dirty bayonet Goldrein - go to the guardroom". One fellow officer-cadet, who had been in Burma and suffered malaria, fainted. He was put on a charge for 'falling out without permission'!

Training was hard. Again we had the ten miles in two hours with full kit, and climbing mountains at night with neither torch nor map. You were returned to your unit - in other words you were no longer on the officer ladder - if you had either. Or, I should say, if you were found with either.

For the 'night in the mountains' I took the precaution of taking both torch and map with me - otherwise I think I would still be wandering lost through the Welsh mountains - but I was not caught. At this distance in time I suppose I am safe. Despite those aids I and my two colleagues were the last to arrive back the next morning.

My map-reading was not of the best. Before going out we had been given a large map to study before we left, and we were allowed to copy it to enable us to return. Apart from that we had our real, unofficial map, too. The pole star, I understood, was north. The trouble was that I with my two mates got the wrong star, with the result that we moved in a large circle. I forget how we got back, but we must have done - otherwise we would still be there. We were so lost that on two occasions we climbed down steep hills expecting to find a route through. Each time we found a fast-flowing river and had to climb to the top and try again. Our torches and map had not helped us a great deal.

We went on 'schemes', which really meant maximum hardship, discomfort and unpleasant living conditions, for three or five days at a time. At the start of one five-day scheme I was the cadet platoon commander for the morning, when we were faced with a stream. It was winter, the officers were watching me to see what I would do, and to check whether or not I was a 'leader of men'. I had tried it at Wosbee and so I thought I would try it here. I decided to set the example, knowing from the past that the water would be only inches deep. "Follow me!", I shouted, and started to run across the stream, a distance of about five yards.

I had not taken into account the effects of winter. The water came up to my neck. I had to hold my rifle above my head to keep it dry as that was far more important than me. I got out at the other side soaked to the skin. Before the others could follow the officer pointed out to them an alternative crossing about a hundred yards or so up the river. I shall never know whether he did this to put me to the test, or out of spite. I spent the five days soaking. My cigarettes, paybook, money, everything, were soaking. We slept one night in a barn full of hay. It was quite warm and soft. The downside was that I dropped something - I think it was a cigarette lighter - and it fell through the hay. It was indeed a case of looking for a lighter in a haystack and I never found it. The extraordinary thing was that I never even got a cold or a sniff. They had at least made me fit.

The conditions on that 'five day scheme' were appalling. In one place, near Bala Lake, very beautiful at any other time, we were advancing against the 'enemy' from whom we were under fire. It was real 'fire' – live bullets coming across, but aimed, fortunately successfully, to go over our heads. One friend of mine got on to his tummy to get away from the covering fire – the real bullets coming too close for comfort. The setting was indeed very realistic and, I suppose, was superb battle training. As he fell his bayonet went into the thigh of the another officer cadet in front of him - Des Perris whom I had known in my Cambridge days - and out the other side. Des was so cold, he told me later, he never even felt it. When he got up the bayonet came out and he kept running until his leg gave way. It was only then that he realised what had happened. The pain was of no consequence. His difficulty was that he was delayed a month in getting his commission as he had to recover in hospital.

They certainly toughened us up. By the time we finished I can fairly say that we could do anything that our men would be able to do, and much more. We were toughened and hardened, we had put up with some eight months in all of extremely arduous training, hostile conditions, a fair amount of danger in the mountains and with the use of live ammunition for verisimilitude - and we managed all this without counselling! These days there would be more counsellors than those to be counselled!

The day came for the 'passing-out parade', our final parade before obtaining our commissions. Regimental Sergeant Major Cop put us through our ceremonial paces, and we would have done credit to Trooping the Colour. My parents were there. A little proud, perhaps, but fearful of what the future held in store for a young and junior infantry officer. I remember my father being troubled because I, his younger son, usually so light hearted, looked so stern and serious during the ceremony. If I had not been so stern and serious I would have been in trouble - Mr Cop had no time for smiles.

We went back to our billet - the Marine Hotel - to change into our officers' uniforms. On went the service dress, smart peaked cap, shoulder flashes, the Sam Browne belt and the twinkling 'pip', the insignia of the second lieutenant (the lowest form of animal life, as Mr Cop described us), and there we were at last.

When I went into the mess room – the words used for the dining room - I momentarily stood to attention thinking I was in the wrong place, because the room was full of officers - until I realised I was one too. But in fact we were only dressed up as officers. Our commissions would not be gazetted until the following day. This was a simple precaution to prevent us from getting our own back on Mr Cop and his team of sergeants who were, in theory, now our subordinates. Otherwise we would have sought them out wherever they were, so that they would have had to stand to attention and salute us.

--oOo--

Chapter 5
A Real Officer

Now at last I was an officer. I could carry a swagger cane or, as an infantry officer, a walking stick. I wonder what people thought of this boy - I indeed looked even less than my age, and I was just 20 anyway - swaggering along the main streets in the centre of Liverpool swinging my walking stick with such authority. I remember seeing a Guardsman coming towards me, over six feet tall, peaked cap, very smart. This was, I thought, going to bring me a really good salute, a privilege to which I was entitled from all non-commissioned ranks. Up he came - but to my dismay, no salute! He just walked past me!

I turned and called peremptorily, 'Soldier'. He turned, came up, and then saluted. 'Sir!', he said. I asked him, although I well knew the answer, 'What is your regiment?'. He replied 'Coldstream Guards sir!'. I replied 'That can't be correct. They salute officers in the Coldstream Guards!'. He apologised, saluted smartly and, with my permission, left. I wonder what he really thought of me, or perhaps it is better not to think.

I enjoyed an excellent seven-day leave, particularly the adulation from the family and congratulations from my friends. I could now see myself leading men into action, brave and fearless, and respected by all not only for myself but for my elevated position - a second lieutenant.

After four days of my leave I received my posting papers. I was to go to a place called Moffat in Dumfriesshire in Scotland, to a Battle School. Was I to be an instructor? Whatever it was it sounded interesting and, as an officer, I would be experiencing the burdens and privileges of leadership and authority, no longer the dogsbody as I been hitherto.

Before going to the Battle School we were posted to Cragside, in Northumberland, I suppose to be sorted out, and this had been the home of the Armstrongs of Vickers Armstrong, the great industrialists and armaments manufacturers. I did not have exactly a bedroom there. I slept on my camp bed in an attic, but it was better than a tent. In the officers' mess we had a proper dining room too.

The ante-room - which we would, I think, call the lounge, although in this case it was as big as a hotel lounge - was very comfortable. But the first evening I went in all the chairs were occupied - bar one, a very comfortable armchair near to a beautiful roaring fire. There was no central heating in those days. I sat down, relaxed and read. The adjutant approached me, and advised me that I was sitting in the colonel's chair, and that although he was not there it was still his chair. I replied that I understood that all officers were equal in the mess and he departed. But I soon realised that some officers are more equal than others, even in the mess.

He won. He arranged that I should be the orderly officer, responsible for keeping the headquarters mess properly running for a number of evenings and nights. This kept me out of the ante-room during the evenings, and fairly tired the next morning from lack of sleep.

One evening I was sleeping on a camp-bed in the adjutant's office, being on duty all night, when inadvertently I knocked over an ink-pot - it was before the days of ball pens. The next morning he 'carpeted' me for this sin and I pointed out that had he followed the normal practice of putting the cap on the ink-pot before leaving the office the previous evening there would have been no problem. I do not know what the consequences would have been, as the adjutant had many powers, but the next day I had to leave for the Battle School - and as a pupil and not a teacher.

We arrived at the battle school. Here were lots of new officers, and all very smart, with suitcases (no longer kit bags where the very thing you wanted was always, by virtue of Murphy's Law, at the bottom) and with a batman to sort us out and to see that we were comfortable. We were back to a kind of barrack room, although not in any way the measure of discomfort to which we had been subjected as 'other ranks'. But, as always, there was a downside - we had to wear denim battle-dress uniforms with no badges of rank. After all those months of striving, working, freezing, being shouted at and practically tortured to get that little 'pip', the insignia of a second-lieutenant, on our shoulders it had to come off again, albeit temporarily.

The next day, rather to our surprise, we were lined up and put on parade - with a sergeant-major sorting us out. The only difference from our previous experience was that he called each of us 'sir', instead of ''orrible cadet'. The word 'sir' sounds good, but the manner in which it was said reduced it to a mocking term of derision. We were then taken to a large training area and told that we were the advancing troops under the cover of an artillery barrage, that the shells would fall within 50 yards in front of us, and that we should get used to the experience. We were in a long shallow trench when the barrage commenced. I was standing next to the colonel - I thought that might be safer.

The shells going over our heads were like the noise of railway engines. These were 25-pounder shells. They roared overhead, landing a matter of fifty yards or so in front of us. I remembered, having served in the Royal Artillery, that we had been told that we were perfectly safe behind the falling shells as the blast and shrapnel went forwards. And so I remained standing. Everybody else got down. Suddenly, from next to my feet was a roar from the colonel, lying flat, "Get down you bloody

fool. You could get killed. What a waste of the cost of your training!".
I got down.

The next day we were to do house-fighting in Leith near Edinburgh, in bombed-out tenements. The battle school had been bad enough hitherto, but this was even worse. The 'enemy' were other ranks but they were dressed in German uniforms. They may not have hated us as Germans would, but they had their chance to get at officers for the only time in their lives and they were not going to miss it.

We were on the broken tiles on the roof-top of a 7-storey tenement. I hate heights, and was terrified. One young officer dropped the magazine from his Sten gun - a small and not very effective sub-machine gun - and it fell to the ground. That was bad enough, but what was worse was the time it took for us to hear it hit the ground - about the same time as it would have taken us to hit the ground if we, as seemed quite likely, suffered the same fate.

We went down from the roof to the top floor. Half of the floorboards were missing. We came to a glassless window and were told to jump across nearly two feet, with all our equipment, to the opposite window on the building next door. That really was a terrifying prospect. I gritted my teeth, and jumped. I found myself in a room full of 'Germans'. I pointed my Sten gun at them and said 'Bang, bang, bang. you're all dead!'. The prompt response was, 'Are we f***!', and about eight of them came for me, knocked me to the ground - and there was a sheer drop, through the missing floorboards, only about a foot away. I was scared and getting punched and kicked when, to my everlasting relief, one of the officers who was an umpire said 'You're dead'. I have never heard a pronouncement with more relief. I was allowed to be restored to life and go back to base. But I had learned a very good lesson – street and house-to-house fighting are very dangerous and were to be avoided at all costs.

We had three weeks of that and I was then posted to a battalion of the Green Howards at Richmond, Yorkshire, a sister regiment of my own regiment, the East Yorkshires. It was a few days before Christmas and there was little to do other than to find my bearings. My first duty was in fact on Christmas Day, when democracy had it that I, together with other junior officers, should act at waiters in the other ranks dining hall, and serve them their meal. So, at last, I had performed my first duty as a real officer.

From there I was posted to the village of Rothbury in Northumberland to take command of a trainee platoon. I, with two other new subalterns, who were to command the other two platoons in the company, were allocated accommodation in one of the local hotels which had been taken over by the army, and there we had very adequate bedrooms - far better accommodation that I had had hitherto in the army or, indeed, at Cambridge, although it was not actually Claridges. We ate in the Officers' mess and we had a batman each to keep the place and our possessions tidy and clean. I really do not know what they did with the rest of the day. I felt that all the hardships had been worthwhile - at last I could enjoy a degree of civilisation. The troops were trainee infantrymen, but then I was in a sense still a trainee officer, as I had never in fact had a real command before. I, and my troops, wore denim battledress, but at last I had a 'pip', the insignia of a second lieutenant, on my shoulder and could wear a tie. I was, before anything else, introduced to my platoon sergeant, Sergeant Hunt - who was the executive arm through whom and with whom I was to run my platoon. He was what you might call my 'second in command'. The difference was that I was to be there for six weeks, to train the platoon, whereas he was a permanent fixture and knew his way round whilst I did not. He was what was called the 'cadre sergeant', and who was the platoon sergeant to each successive platoon and each successive new second-lieutenant. He did not wear denim overalls - he wore a proper battledress, which was far more formal and impressive. In truth he was not only training the men but he was training me too. It was quite a delicate situation.

I felt it would be better to have a good working relationship with him, realising that as he knew all the ropes having done it all before many times, and as I knew no ropes at all, he could make my task easier or very difficult, if he so chose. That being so I, the first evening, invited him to the local pub for a friendly drink in the bar. Of course in those days he still called me 'sir', even socially, and he was Sergeant Hunt. We had a pleasant drink and a chat, and that effort certainly in due course served me extremely well.

The next day the colonel came to speak to me. He had heard that I had had a drink with the sergeant, and really thought that it was inappropriate for an officer to fraternise with an N.C.O., even just for a drink. I think it was then that again the streak of the rebel came to the fore, and I answered, very politely of course, that, off duty, there was no reason why I should not have a drink with my sergeant and that there had been no breach of the rules of discipline. I added that – 'with respect' (which always means 'without respect') - I would do it again if I saw fit. To my pleasant surprise he accepted that. Had he not, I feel sure that the report he would have put in could have done me no good.

In the course of our training - I was new as an officer and the men were new as men (although really all of us were boys) - we went out, naturally, on exercises. One late evening we were out on the Moors, the rain was raining, the cold was cold, and the wind was windy and the dark was dark. We were shortly going out on patrol to reconnoitre to see if there was any enemy around - apart from the weather.

There was some delay and with the conditions in mind I gave my platoon, some thirty men in all, permission to have their evening meal. The surroundings were not five star and there was not exactly a white table cloth off which to eat – not, indeed, even a table, let alone a chair. However it warmed the inner man and we tucked in. The repast was not exactly cordon bleu - it was in fact dry rations to be eaten out of a not-too-clean mess tin. Nevertheless I had rarely enjoyed a meal more. And then we were rudely interrupted. The Colonel came up and demanded to know why we were eating. I explained that we were hungry and cold. He told me that I should be rehearsing my platoon. I replied that they would rehearse better on full stomachs (he clearly had never heard of Napoleon) - perhaps hardly the way for a young second-lieutenant to speak to the colonel. He then challenged me and accused me: "You are a murderer! You should be rehearsing the patrol". I replied that the alternative would have been to die of hunger. With that he turned on his heel and left.

As a digression, some years later, back in England, I was the officer in charge of re-embarkation of troops on to a troopship in Liverpool to return to India from leave. I was in my office on the dockside when an irate colonel came in, demanding a better cabin to be consistent with his rank. I recognised the same colonel. Although I had no choice in the allotment of cabins, and it was too late to change anyway, it gave me considerable pleasure to tell him that unfortunately nothing could be done and that he should get aboard as the ship was to sail any minute. He was almost too angry to reply - perhaps he noticed that my tone was not exactly warm. And then - and Nemesis does strike - I had the pleasure of saying to him, "And there is just one more thing Colonel, and that is that I was the young officer you called a murderer for not rehearsing his patrol at Catterick some time ago. None died on the patrol despite the lack of rehearsal. And you had better return to the ship - Sir!". It was the first time I had actually seen anyone speechless.

We became very competitive with this training battalion. There were three of us, young new officers, each leading a platoon, and each vying with the others to be the best platoon. The troops were all new to their job, and each of us tried to instil into them the fact that we had to win. The three of us - the officers - were good friends and the rivalry was always clean and with no sharp edges. My platoon was ultimately given the accolade, but I am sure - and this is not modesty - it was by the shortest head.

It was during this period I had another experience mixing with 'other ranks': I discovered that one of the men - although we were really all just boys - was from my old school, Hymers. He was in another platoon and one afternoon after exercises I popped in to their barrack room to have a chat with him. I sat on his bunk, we reminisced for about 10 minutes, spoke about our army lives and our hopes for our civilian futures, and then I got up to leave. I had not noticed before then that all the men - apart from my friend - were standing, and when I stood up they all came to attention. Such was the rule and the way of life in those days that the mere presence of an officer, however junior, was sufficient to bring about that reaction. I felt most embarrassed to have inconvenienced them and told them to 'stand at ease', and left, no doubt much to their relief.

And so after preliminary training, corps training, Pre-Officer Cadet Training Unit, O.C.T.U., Battle School, the training battalion and the rest, we were at last considered sufficiently trained to be of use. We had one week's leave which, of course, I spent at home with the family, and then I had to leave on a posting abroad. We were not told where we were going but clearly one had an idea of a number of countries and places which could be involved and so my parents and I worked out a set of codes: I think a reference to 'tea' was India, and the only other one I can clearly remember was Somalia. This was a very unlikely long shot but I looked at the map, at all the possible places, and some of the impossible, where I might be sent, and coded them all. I remember Somalia because my grandparents lived in Somali Road in Cricklewood, and so all I had to do if that were appropriate was to mention 'Grandpa and Grandma'.

I had first to go to London, and my mother arranged that she should stay with her parents - in Somali Road - in case there was a chance to see me before I left. She, of course, travelled direct but I had to travel to London via Catterick in Yorkshire, my battalion headquarters. My father saw me off at the station in Liverpool. He was, as usual, immaculate, a single-breasted coat with a fly front and an 'Anthony Eden' hat, very much the fashion then. He was a lovely man. We found it hard to conceal our emotions but we managed. I was never to see him again. To this day I remember him so clearly standing there, keeping a brave face, and I do not know how either of us held back the tears, except that in those days one was not allowed to show emotions.

My parents were far from happy. My brother Eric, an officer in the Royal Artillery, had been wounded soon after the Normandy landings, and now the 'baby of the family' was about to go abroad to an unknown destination, and to face the dangers of sailing across the Atlantic and whatever was to follow. The shipping losses had been enormous but at last we had come to a time when it was far less dangerous, so I encouraged my mother and myself.

After a few days - too few - I received orders to report to King's Cross station to board a train to Greenock, near Glasgow, there to embark. My mother came with me in the taxi to the station, and as I got out I told her to drive off rather than having the trauma - for both of us - of each slowly disappearing in the other's eyes. She drove off in the taxi, I waved as cheerfully as I could, and then made my way to the platform.

When I got to the platform I had no doubt that I, with the other officers, would be travelling first class, whilst the other ranks would be travelling in third class - there was no second class in those days. I should really have been used to shocks by now: I found that the whole train was third class and that I was supposed to be in charge of the troops. Little me and dozens, or perhaps hundreds, of men, and I was to control them! At one stop they all got out to go to the station shop to buy chocolates or cigarettes although they had all received orders before we left that they should not leave the train. I did not even try to get them back on the train as I would have been a voice in the wilderness. But when the train whistled and very slowly started to move they all came aboard. Otherwise I suppose I would have been in trouble.

We complain about trains today, but we were in a different world. First of all the trains were steam drawn, and so there was smoke and soot, very slow acceleration and fairly slow stopping - and so if the train had to stop at a signal for any reason it seemed to take for ever to get its speed up again. Also being a special train as opposed to a scheduled service – although in wartime schedules meant little - it was even slower. A journey which today would, I suppose, take about four hours and a bit took about nine. Eventually we drew up at the dockside of Greenock, and there awaiting us was the armed merchant cruiser on which we were to embark, the 'Celicia', a pre-war liner with a displacement of about twelve thousand tons. That was quite substantial in those days.

An 'armed merchant cruiser' meant that she sailed on her own and not in a convoy, because of her greater speed. She had a fairly large gun at the rear to deal with submarines.

Here, I thought, that at last my rank would help me, at least in accommodation - but by now my optimism was, rightly as it proved, fading.

All the passengers were officers and, of course, although all officers were in theory equal, some were more equal than others. As a junior subaltern I was the lowest form of animal, or officer, life. I expected at least a cabin, nevertheless - perhaps to be shared with another second-lieutenant. We were in fact accommodated in a large area which I suppose had once been a recreation area, equipped with 'standees' - a bunk arrangement, one above the other. Unlike normal bunks on a ship, most of them were not against a wall - or bulkhead - but were standing independently. This meant, of course, that there was no place for one's baggage. We had a suitcase each, and so as there were two of us in each standee, there were two suitcases - our wardrobes - underneath each standee. Washing and toilet facilities were to match. Our large tin trunks were put in the hold.

--oOo--

The journey was to the unknown - it became known to us only when we were on board. We were going, first, to Alexandria, Egypt. Of course we were unable to tell the family as there were, in those days, no mobile 'phones. Because there was still the danger of being attacked we had to sail right across the Atlantic, until we were almost within spitting distance of the United States, then go south and back again to the Mediterranean via the Straits of Gibraltar.

There were, of course, lots of life-boat drills, and we took those seriously because they were serious. We ate indifferent food, washed in indifferent showers, and filled our time as best we could. We played a fair amount of bridge, but as there were only two of us who could play we had to teach another two to make up the four. We were honest, and really did tell them the rules. Also I had by then been informed that I was going to be posted to East Africa, and I was given a book called 'Teach Yourself KiSwahili', the language which was supposed to take you from Capetown to Cairo. I knuckled down to it and, by the time we ultimately arrived at our final destination some months later, I was reasonably proficient in the language. Being an old tribal language it has a very involved grammar but, as it only became a written language, so it seems, when the British colonised those parts, we used English characters, which certainly made things easier. By the end of the voyage we could converse in it although not to the extent of involved political or metaphysical discussions, but these were unlikely to be necessary.

One day there was an order that we should have Physical Training on deck every day. It was cold, windy, wet and mid-Atlantic, and so stripping down to singlet and shorts and to stand doing exercises on the open deck was a most unattractive proposition. However in the closed environment of the ship you could not get out of it. It was then I had one of those very rare flashes of brilliance - I volunteered to be the instructor. My offer was gladly accepted. The first day came and those who were doing the P.T., and there were a lot of them, from the rank of major downward, went on to the very cold deck to be put through their paces.

I saw no point in the instructor, who was after all instructing and was not there to partake in the physical training, wearing singlet and shorts, and so I turned up in full kit, hat, gloves, boots, scarf and warm overcoat. I shouted my instructions and discipline having been drilled in to all of us, of all ranks, they immediately moved to the orders of this very junior officer. If I needed to demonstrate any exercise - like, say, a press-up - which it would have been difficult to do fully clothed, I called out one of the other officers, who were more properly clad than I was, to demonstrate what the others should do. Not only did I get away with it, but nobody even objected. I suppose that was because there had to be somebody to be in charge, and there was no obvious reason why he should strip down.

And so with KiSwahili, bridge, and physical training we continued on our journey of about three weeks until we reached the comparative safety of the Straits of Gibraltar. But there was one great day as we crossed the Atlantic, particularly as it made our safe arrival far more likely. News came through that the Germans and their allies had surrendered unconditionally. Save for the odd rogue who may not have got the message, we were safe from torpedoes and our families in the U.K. were safe. My brother was fighting in Europe and so I knew that he was safe too. The only cloud on the horizon was that as we were going east, and as Japan had not surrendered, there was no doubt as to where we were heading. The war was, for us, still very much a reality.

We ultimately came into Alexandria harbour, to find ourselves surrounded by small boats, their crews being Egyptians who were trying to sell us things - anything and everything. We lowered ropes with bags or nets to pick up our purchases, and then lowered the money by the same means. They knew enough English to outwit us on price. We feared that if we had lowered the money first we would never have enjoyed completing the purchase.

From the ship we boarded a train which was to take us to Cairo. A vendor came round with oranges and bananas, which we immediately bought as we had seen neither for quite some time, when John Allen, the medical officer, came to warn us that even fruit could cause us problems as one did not know where it had been grown or how it had been stored, so out that went. We were offered Spanish Fly, apparently a well-known aphrodisiac, but we felt that that was one commodity which we would not need. We were, after all, healthy young men - and clean in body and mind! And then the train pulled out.

The train was slow. Eventually we arrived in Cairo and were taken to the Abbassiya Barracks, a large barracks full of people coming and going and whilst the accommodation was clean and dry, it was no more than a camp bed in a room shared with two or three others.

Being the army, although I am sure that we were expected – there must have been some paper-work about us somewhere – there were naturally no provisions for us to be dealt with immediately or even expeditiously. When one considers the cost of 'running' a highly and expensively trained officer, per day, not only his pay but his rations, accommodation, general servicing, and multiplying this by the number of us there, we were costing the country a lot of money.

That really, though, was not our concern. Until they decided what to do with us our time was our own, and Cairo was our oyster. Naturally the first call was to the pyramids and the Sphinx. He, or perhaps it should it be she, had its head supported by sandbags in case any bombs fell which could have damaged the supporting stone. We hired some ponies – there were three of us – and, wearing our 'slouch' hats - the same as the Australians - we looked every bit like cowboys as we rode round and declined offers to ride on camels, buy food, have our shoes cleaned or utilise the services of the vendors' 'sisters' – their polite way of saying 'ladies of ill-repute'.

Nearby was the Auberge des Pyramides, a fine hotel with a restaurant and dance floor. The war had not really touched Cairo and after so many years with all the privations at home it was quite extraordinary to be walking about with no fear of bombs, no black-out, and no rationing. There were other dangers though – the pick-pockets, shop owners who would try to get you into the back shop and then hold you to ransom, and the constant and continuing offers of sale of 'sisters'. I am glad to say that none of us took advantage of those offers - I would like to think that was because of our high moral standards, but there had also been the warnings of the medical officer.

We went to see the Mohammed Ali mosque, one of the most famous in the Middle East. There were three or four of us. The 'dragomen' or official guides clad in long blue robes and a fez, offered their services but we did not trust them and anyway did not feel inclined to pay what seemed to us to be high fees for their 'guidance'. We continued to look round the magnificent building on our own. We were approached by an Egyptian, probably in his early twenties, impeccably dressed in European-type clothes, and speaking perfect English. He explained that he was a student on vacation, owed a debt to the British for saving his country from the Germans, and offered to show us round. It was an offer which clearly was on a very different basis from that of the official guides.

He was excellent, and I whispered to my friends that this fellow really deserved a tip but that it could be embarrassing to offer money to a type such as that. He continued to show us round and the grand finale was to go right to the top of one of the minarets up a spiral staircase. It gave us a wonderful view of the City and of the rest of the mosque below us. Having seen all we needed to see we decided to go down the spiral staircase, still wondering how we were to reward our guide.

Our problem was soon solved. As we started to move towards the spiral staircase he told us how much we owed him – far more than the dragoman had suggested. We were aghast. I said that we would pay him when we got down as clearly we would have more space to argue and could always walk away. We were four and he was one. Then he played his trump card: He told us that he was not coming down, and his eyes went to the top of the narrow, rather dangerous, long spiral staircase. If he stayed up and we went down we felt that our descent could be rather precipitate - one small push to the last to leave and there would have been without doubt some broken limbs at the very least. We paid. We had learned a lesson.

Unfortunately those in charge discovered that we were where we were, and decided that it would be no doubt cheaper if we were to be moved to a tented camp just outside Suez. That may sound romantic but six or eight officers in a bell tent, sleeping on camp beds but otherwise on the sand, and with all the crawlies, large and small, which one finds in the desert – and it was desert – was no fun. The sun was merciless as summer approached and the only reasonable building was the officers' mess where we could relax and eat: But even there, there were problems. One day an enormous tarantula spider, literally the size of a large hand, was walking towards us across the floor. Someone – certainly not me – had the courage to get it to crawl on to a large piece of wood, and take it outside. Or so we thought. A few moments later, as we sat eating our dessert, he suddenly pushed this enormous creature under our noses –

fortunately it remained on the piece of wood - and, to our great relief, after some pressure from us, he took it away.

What worried me was that the tarantula might be married. I was right – a few minutes later its wife – or husband – came walking across the floor of the mess. One officer had the courage to jump on it and kill it to a horrible squelch. There appeared to be no children.

On a smaller scale were the scorpions – horrible creatures which seemed to find our tent a good resting place. In these conditions I really wondered what difference it had made by being an officer – there could hardly have been less attractive conditions however low one's rank. This went on for what seemed ages. But was probably about three weeks. The only brighter spot was that my promotion to Lieutenant, from Second-Lieutenant, came through, and so my shoulder did not look quite so bare and I did not look quite so junior.

We had other luxuries there to match the bell-tents. These were the toilet facilities. The Romans had done it far better – at least they had flush downs. The ones we had consisted of seats with holes in – naturally - and there was sand below, not water, open at the rear so that the Egyptian 'sweepers' could clear them before they got too smelly. One problem was that some of the sweepers had a rather perverse sense of humour. Realising that we could not see them through the parts of our anatomies covering the holes in the seats they felt free to tickle certain parts of our anatomies with twigs. To say the least they made us jump, not only because of the sudden surprise but in case the twig became sharper, with the added possibility of us singing soprano in the choir.

We did manage to get a short leave, for about three days, and had a choice of the Lakes or Cairo, and I chose the latter with some friends. We could not afford to stay at the famous Shepherd's Hotel, and settled for sharing a room in the National Hotel. It seemed quite good save that one night, tired out and pulling back the covers to get into bed, my eyes rested on a nest of enormous cockroaches comfortably settled in the middle. Not only did we make the hotel staff take my bed apart to ensure that they had cleared them all, but they did the other beds as well just to make sure. The problem was that, having enjoyed my bed once, they may have had an inner desire to return to their former residence.

And then at last our posting orders came: I was to go, with some of the others, to Kenya. We happily gathered our bags and went on board a troopship, the 'Worcestershire'. This was even worse than the first ship, in that we slept in hammocks and there was fresh water only for drinking. We washed in salt water with special soap, but the result was a constant feeling of prickly sticky sweat. This 'luxury' cruise took us from Suez to the main port of Kenya, Mombasa.

Mombasa then was not Mombasa now: It was a run-down scruffy port, no seasides, no amenities. Our bags – and us – were promptly unloaded on to a train – a long train powered by a powerful Garrett locomotive, an enormous engine with a tender at each end to give it enough fuel for the long and steep run to Nairobi, which is a city some several thousand feet above sea-level. Whilst not comfortable it was an improvement, the scenery was fabulous, with a view of Mount Kenya, almost a perfect pyramid, in the distance. The 'stations' on the way were short stops and, of course, without platforms.

Immediately we arrived at any of those stations vendors arrived too, trying to sell us anything available, mostly fruit, and by the standards to which we were accustomed, exotic. They were not like the Egyptian vendors – no 'sisters' were on offer and we felt we could trust them. It was a colourful, pleasant journey, which I remember with pleasure as a highlight after travelling many thousands of miles living in hardly 5-, 4-, 3-, 2-, or even 1-Star accommodation.

Nairobi was a delightful city, small but clean and, in the European centre, attractive. Of course colour at that time was everything, and Africans slept and lived in mud and wattle thatched huts, well away from the better European areas. Buses were divided as to blacks and whites, as were park seats – indeed in every aspect where there could be racial discrimination, there was. There was an Officers' Club in

Delamere Avenue – now known as Kenyatta Avenue – and I had a beer. I gave the 'boy' – the title given to every African servant, whatever his age – a tip of three pence, a very small tip compared with English standards. I thought I was being pretty mean until a brother officer, who was from Nairobi, shouted 'It's you buggers from home who ruin these people!'. I asked what I had done wrong, and he told me in no uncertain terms that a halfpenny – and that is worth less than the new half-pennies of today, if we still had them - was more than enough.

We were accommodated in Langata Transit Camp, each with a room of his own – not luxurious, but a damn sight better than that to which we had become accustomed – and the days were spent looking round, socialising with the locals and enjoying the relaxation. During that time I met a girl called Gilla Lustman, a nice pretty girl, and we went to a dance together and I was invited to her home. I must have met her two or three times. Many years later – in the late eighties – I found myself in contact with a man called Harold Lustman from Kenya, but who was in London on business. I asked him if he was related to Gilla, and he told me that she was his sister, living now in South Africa, and was a widow. I told him that I had met her and bantered that it was fortunate that I had been a good boy, as otherwise he might have challenged me as being the father of any illegitimate children! He was not amused. But it is a small world!

Indeed my expectation, from the moment I knew I was going to East Africa, was that I would probably be sent to Burma with the 11th East African Division. I was not keen on fighting Japanese in Burma – nobody was – and still less with black troops because, as the only white man, I would clearly be the officer and the first target. Also the only language between me and my troops would have been Swahili – as KiSwahili was better known - and that was not quite my mother tongue. Not a nice thought. I was due to be given my 'posting' any day. Then one morning I saw newspaper placards which read 'Equivalent of 40,000 tons of bombs dropped on Japan' – the news of the first atomic bomb on Hiroshima. I was pleased to read that the Japanese, after all their cruelties, were having a bashing. Then, I think it was four days later, there was another one – this time on Nagasaki. News followed fast and suddenly we heard that the Japanese were petitioning for peace. It was incredible. I knew that wherever I was sent it must have been to somewhere not as bad a Burma. Whatever people say about the rights and wrongs of the first nuclear bombs, I have no doubt that they were right. On a personal level they certainly saved me from tremendous hardship, mutilation or death. That applied to millions of others, British and American, and after the Japanese atrocities throughout that theatre of war I had no doubt that hundreds of thousands of Allied lives had been saved by those bombs, possibly including mine.

So what was going to happen to me now? I did not have to wait long: I was told to attend before a committee of three senior officers – I remember that the Chairman was Colonel Lord Francis, a cousin of the then Queen - and I duly went to be interviewed. They asked all details of my background and I 'modestly' mentioned the fact that I had a degree in Law. I felt it might help. That was, I suppose, enough for the Army to put two and two together and to reach five. They realised the Law had something to do with police, and gendarmes were police in a sense, so they decided to send me to the Somalia Gendarmerie. I had no idea what that was, but it had to be better than Burma would have been. And I had the code word to tell my parents where I was going.

--oOo--

Chapter 6
The Place God Forgot

The Somalia Gendarmerie was short of vehicles so it was arranged that four 15 cwt (the abbreviation for 'hundredweight' in those days) trucks should be driven up to Mogadishu , the capital, from Nairobi with four African drivers, and with a British officer in each, so that we could travel not too uncomfortably.

On the first part of the journey there was a measure of civilisation. We went through the little town of Nanyuki, where there were quite a few whites, and I remember there a pub – so English that we could have been at home – called the Silver Beck. There was a white line across the floor of the main bar, and that was the equator, which you crossed as you carried your beer from the bar to the table, or when you visited the loo. Another small but pleasant town was Neri, but after that the roads and townships ran out.

For the first fifty miles or so we drove along made roads, but then the roads ran out. There were tracks – one knew where to drive because there were tyre marks and you could see where the track was worn, but every now and again we came to a wadi. They were fortunately dry –

it would have been difficult otherwise as there were no bridges. Our drivers drove at them as if it part of the normal 'road', with the result my truck, being the first one, got stuck in the middle of the wadi. The others were still alright. We then had to use the other vehicles to pull mine out so that all four were still on normal ground level.

We then decided that we would be the drivers and our drivers would be our passengers. The system we adopted was, of course, to drive at speed down one bank and up the other, taking a good run at it so as not to be stuck on the dry river bed. We went at each one like a racing driver and came out unscathed.

One problem was dust and sand thrown up by the vehicles in front. For this reason we took it in turns to lead. It was so thick that sometimes one could not see through the windscreen, as this was well before the invention of screen washers. If one tried to drive with the windscreen open to let some air in one became covered with a complete film of dust and sand.

We stopped for meals – we had taken rations and adequate water with us for the five-day journey. It was at one of these breaks that we realised that the wild life could well constitute a very pleasant evening dinner. The main problem was that the wild life we were after – buck, antelopes, oryx and many more - tended to come out early in the morning or as dusk came down, the day time being on the hot side which they obviously preferred to avoid. The fiercer animals were pretty well completely absent during the day, but there were some buck about.

Our soldiers were equipped with army Lee-Enfield rifles. I borrowed one and got our first oryx fairly quickly during the first late afternoon, and so we decided then to encamp for the night and ordered our four 'other ranks' to prepare the repast. They lit a fire, more or less by rubbing two boy scouts together, and soon had the oryx ready for the 'oven'. The side dishes came from our rations. The accoutrements were not exactly the Ritz.

The oryx was excellent, and oryx liver a delicacy which I can recall to this day. We realised that in those temperatures there was not going to be any storage period, and so what we were unable to eat could be left behind for the vultures or jackals. So when the 'table' was cleared, the uneaten parts were taken a little way from our encampment, and within minutes there were vultures in the few trees, and a moment later they were on the oryx remains. The jackals were not far behind and really before you could say 'knife' only the bones were left.

Our men then lit a good fire, as dusk was coming down, and we ordered them to have a sentry rota so that they could ensure that the fire remained on. This was not to keep us warm but to stop jackals or, indeed, other wild life, taking too much interest in us.

The next morning, as dawn broke, we were off. It was in all a fascinating journey, with an occasional tribesman walking past from nowhere to nowhere. We saw very few settlements, but there was wild life of all kinds getting out of our way. All we needed, but did not have, was a camera. They were simply, and quite properly, not allowed in the armed forces. They were not, of course, the tiny cameras of today which one might be able to hide, but great big things which would have been very obvious.

This went on for about four days, and then we came across what was, by comparison, a degree of civilisation. The track led us to the Juba River, which we had to cross, and which had a rickety ferry, wooden, worked by the locals, which could take one of our trucks at a time. They sang as they pulled it across, and it was almost a 'Ol' Man River' scene. But get us across they did, and then we drove off again.

Our pattern of driving, eating and drinking and sleeping remained much the same as at the start, and we allowed our drivers to drive occasionally lest we fell asleep. And then in the distance we saw the target, the City of Mogadishu, the capital of Somalia, and we felt that at last we would be back to the degree of civilisation which one could or might expect from a capital city.

Mogadishu

This was – and still is - the capital city of Somalia, or Italian Somaliland as it was called in those days. It was a colonial capital city built by the Italians. Well, the description 'one horse' might be a bit too good for it. There was one main road, a central Police Station, a mosque and a few shops. The road was paved but that was about all. The surrounding areas were shacks and shanties. The only decent building in the 'city' was the former Italian Viceroy's residence, the Duke of Aosta's Palace, which was used as the Headquarters Mess and offices. This was quite grand and stood out in stark contrast to everything else. I slept there the night of my arrival and had breakfast in quite a magnificent dining room but then I had to settle down at the place where I was based, which was the Central Police Station.

The Gendarmerie was a mixture of police and occupying army. Our cap-badge consisted of dik-dik horns – the horns of a very small buck, about the size of a large rabbit, set into a silvery badge with the letters 'SG', Somalia Gendarmerie, engraved on it. It was quite attractive but pride, shortly afterwards, made me shoot my own with a 303 service rifle when I was up-country. The target was moving and small but I got it first go and wore it with some pride. In fact when I ultimately returned to the U.K. I always wore that cap-badge about which I could always say, with my hand on my heart, that I had shot it myself. These days they would have shot me for killing preserved game.

The Italians had surrendered some time ago and were now on our side. This left the British with a problem – what could they do with experienced Italian army officers who were now redundant? They decided, and it was not a bad idea, to make them Warrant Officers – quite a demotion – to serve under us. I therefore found myself with two Italian warrant officers who were in fact very good and served me well. The only problem was that of language, but somehow I managed to get a book called 'Teach Yourself Italian' – I must have got it from an officer who was leaving – and I worked hard on it. Within a week or two I could make myself understood and it has stood me in good stead since. With this and my Swahili I was now ready and prepared.

I was due to be sent up-country to look after an area of some hundreds of square miles and to keep it free from marauding tribes who had a nasty habit of cutting the women about after doing that which they presumably intended to do in the first place, and of cutting off certain rather vital parts of the men and putting them into their mouths – the poor men were usually dead by then, fortunately for them. However in the meantime a temporary job came up and they decided, I suppose for once not unreasonably on paper, that it was just for me.

Clearly as I had a law degree I knew something about the Law – this was clearly the philosophy, and not unreasonably. They assumed, and again not unreasonably, that I was familiar with the courts. Little did they know that at Cambridge I had learned all the niceties of the law, the history, backgrounds and philosophy, but I had never been in or near a court in my life – indeed I had never even been in to a solicitor's office. But they were not to know that.

A chap called 'Dizzy' Tron was the officer who prosecuted in the British Military Administration Court. He was away on leave and so who, they must have thought, was more appropriate than me to take his place for the couple of months before he came back? And so the next morning I turned up at court – the first one I had ever seen. It was rather like a standard English magistrates' court, but then courts the world over look much the same. The 'judge' was rather like a stipendiary magistrate – although nowadays they call them District Judges – and he was a Major Atherton. My job was to prosecute, and there were several local Italian lawyers who sometimes defended those who were accused of some crime.

When I heard that Major Atherton was in charge, and he was, after all, a brother British officer, I went round to his chambers to introduce myself and we had a coffee together. We continued to do this all the time I was there. Looking back on it, it really must have looked most extraordinary to the public and lawyers that here was the prosecutor, at the end of each case, popping into the 'judge's' chambers to have a coffee and a chat. Imagine doing that in England!

Justice may have been done but it certainly would not appear to have been done. The curious thing – and I only thought about this afterwards – was that nobody took any exception to it. I suppose that the Somalis would not have known and it seems that the Italians considered it to be a normal part of the process.

I knew nothing about giving an opening address to the Court so that the judge or, in this case, the Resident Magistrate, Major Atherton, would have had some idea of what it was all about. For the first few days, until I realised that an opening address was very useful, I just called my witnesses and let them tell the story. It was not, of course, as easy as that. It never is. The witnesses spoke in either Swahili or Somali, and there was an interpreter. I knew enough Swahili to check on that and I was frequently quite astonished at the mis-translations. It could well have been as the result of a greased palm, but I had no proof. When it came to the Somali language I was stuck and there was nothing I could do about it. I was not sure either – and I am still not sure – how much Swahili Atherton knew. He certainly knew no Somali.

And so I called my witnesses, and then the defendants, some of whom were represented by the Italian advocates, followed with their witnesses. Again at that time I had no knowledge of closing speeches, and it appeared that some of the Italian advocates had little knowledge of them either, but if ever they gave a closing address I followed them, not to be outdone, by giving my closing address and nobody objected. As it happened I was doing the right thing as the prosecutor is always entitled to the last word.

Punishments could sometimes be immediate. I clearly recall a youth been sentenced to six strokes of the cane. I forget the offence. That may on the face of it not sound bad, but to see it was rather a different experience. The youth was made to lie down on the ground, and a great big African sergeant, in immaculate khaki uniform and fez, stood over him, cane in his right hand, and measured up. And then he gave the caning. I had thought that my old headmaster was tough, although it never happened to me, but this made that look like child's play. At the end of that punishment I think he would have been a reformed character. It is no longer a law that is applied here, but there may be some who consider that it would not be a bad idea.

I could make mistakes too – but some at least could be glossed over. Some could not. One day a defendant called Mohamed Ali was called to the dock, charged with urinating in the street. I gave an opening address – I had learnt the art by then. I said that the defendant had been caught urinating in the street. Concise, but it covered all the relevant circumstances. He pleaded guilty. He was sentenced to a fine of, I think, five East African shillings, about the same as the same sum in England then, and today would be quite a few pounds.

A case or two later - it was a case of larceny - I called one of my witnesses, Mohamed Ali. He took the oath and then I intended to take him through his evidence as set out in his statement – or at least I tried to. He failed completely to 'come up to proof'. He knew, so he said, nothing about the incident. I was thinking of having him prosecuted for perjury, or to ask for him to be committed for contempt of court.

Then I suddenly realised the problem. I had muddled up the two Mohamed Alis. I realised later that it was quite a common name. The one who had pleaded guilty to urinating in the street had in fact been the theft case witness, but had quite reasonably answered to his name when called in the first case of the day. I suppose that he had urinated in the street as most men did – there were no public toilets – and had not realised that he had been seen, and so had pleaded guilty. The Mohamed Ali I had called as a witness was the real urinator.

I do not know if there is any procedure to deal with such a problem. The fine ordered against the first one had already been recorded and the money paid. The conviction had to be expunged and the money repaid. I left it to the clerical and court staff to sort that one out whilst I got on with the theft case, and this time called the right Mohamed Ali as the witness.

One morning before the first trial started I was glancing through my papers and found that the first case was one where one group of prostitutes had been fighting with a competing group – perhaps they had been invading each others' territories. In any case the charge was of affray or something similar. I glanced at the dock and saw a large number of these women jostling and awaiting trial. I glanced through my papers – I never read them until the morning of the trial, but that was because I only received them as I went into court. There was a little parcel with the papers with a label on which was written 'Exhibit A'. I was in the course of opening it and at the same time glanced at the file. There I read – 'Exhibit A, One Lower Lip'! I hastily dropped the little parcel and looked towards the dock. I could see precisely from which mouth the exhibit had come. Poor woman, that must have cramped her style for future commercial enterprises.

I was from England, and so my background was not colonial. One of my brother officers was called Jay York. He was from Rhodesia, and to make it worse he had been in the Rhodesian Police Force, which was called, for reasons which I could not fathom, The British South African Police. He was in command of the East Police Station. I popped in one day to see how he was and to have a cup of tea. Whilst I was there a suspect was brought in – I forget the charges of which he was suspected. To my utter surprise and horror Jay ordered two or three of his men to push the suspect's head down between his legs, while he was still standing, and then made him, by putting his arms behind his knees, hold his ears – an extremely uncomfortable position. He was made to hold that position whilst Jay questioned him and questioned him. He got no answers – one reason could be that the suspect was not guilty, but that never, I am sure, entered into Jay's contemplation.

So he tried the next interrogation technique: The suspect was made to lie on his back and his mouth was held open. Then water was poured into his mouth until he nearly choked. That failed. Jay then brought a rhino whip out of his safe and started to beat him – still with no success. With that he ordered his men to take him out to lock him up, calmly went to the safe on the way, took out a bottle of mehtylated spirits to clean his hands, wiped them, and then carried on with the cup of tea. I was shocked then and I am shocked now. I am glad I was never infected by that particular colonial bug. When I challenged Jay about it he could not understand me any more than I could understand him.

My time as prosecutor lasted for about two months, and very useful and entertaining it was too, but eventually Dizzy Tron returned from leave and they had to find another job for me. I met Dizzy on his return and there was an immediate mutual friendship. Very many years later, when I was senior partner in my firm, I did all the employment law and industrial tribunals. One day I was on the telephone to the personnel advisor in a big firm – I have forgotten if we were on the same side or opponents – and I was told that I was being put through to Mr Tron. It was an unusual name. I asked if he was Dizzy, and indeed he was. We arranged to meet but most unfortunately he died not long afterwards and so we never had the opportunity to compare notes.

I then had to spend a few days lazing about, and there was little to do in Mogadishu. However one of my Italian sergeant majors told be that he could arrange to have a private car available for me if I was interested without any rental payments and with no obligations. Of course I was interested. There was a weekly bus service, if you can call it that, to Nairobi, which was run by an Italian called Rihani. I was told that the Rihanis would be happy to have a car available for me – self-drive – if I so wished. Sleaze had not entered into the language at that time, and as Rihani was never involved in any cases there I felt that there was no harm in my having the car and so I took it. It was the equivalent of the then Austin 7, a little Lancia, but it was very useful.

One day I received an invitation from Mrs Rihani to visit her house for tea. When I got there I found that there were just the two of us, her husband being on his way to or from Nairobi. We had a pleasant tea on the veranda served by her many servants, and after that I thanked her for the tea and the car before going on my way. Just before I left she showed me round the house, which was spacious with lounges and large bedrooms. I was about 20 and she was in her mid- to late twenties, so she was, to me, a little old and I treated her as one would treat an older person, with all proper respect. I thanked her for her hospitality and then off I drove. It was only when one of the Italian sergeant-majors mentioned it to me later that I realised what she had really wanted, or, to put it another way, what I had missed! I must have been a young innocent and very naive, but I am glad I was. I still kept the car until I was moved from Mogadishu.

Another way of passing time was 'going to the seaside'. That consisted of a wooden shed on the deserted beach, because that part of the beach was for whites only, and there was not many whites. The sea was warm and lovely, but the sun was dangerously, very dangerously, hot. We knew this only too well because the sand was too hot to walk on and we had no sandals in our kit. They were not the sort of things you brought out from England, and those we could have purchased locally, as worn by the locals, were not really suitable for European feet. The only answer was to throw a towel in front of you, walk on it, throw another one in front of you, pick up the one behind you, and do the same again until you got to the water, and then the towels went on to your shoulders until you were fully submerged apart from your head.

There was a 21st party arranged for me by the colonel during this period. There were about eight of us and they made it a memorable occasion. The colonel was 'Dicky' Bird, a delightful man, and my closest colleague was Ted Percival who ran the training school. To go back a little, it was Ted who was in theatre in civilian life and who put on a pantomime - Cinderella – whilst I was doing my prosecuting, and I played the part of the good witch. A local dentist blacked out some of my teeth so that I looked even more horrible and managed to develop the appropriate cackle. There was one Italian woman who was heard to remark that it was a great pity that such a young man should have lost so many teeth. The pantomime was a roaring success, and although I cannot recall precisely I think that the audience must have included the locals as there were hardly enough whites to fill even a small theatre.

--oOo--

Chapter 7
The Desert Rat

When Dizzy Tron came back they had to find another job for me. I was sent up to Villagio Duca Delli Abruzzi – known locally as Villabruzzi. As I have mentioned, the Duke of Abruzzi had been a previous Italian viceroy and the village was named after him. It was a full day's drive from Mogadishu. I had a Company of Somali troops and a Ugandan sergeant-major, who was very large and tough – indeed he look very much like Idi Amin whom you will recall was involved in the Entebbe Raid. He was excellent.

The language was Swahili. The troops lived in mud huts with straw roofs. I had a brick bungalow with most mod. cons. including a bathroom and loo, and three personal servants – not just a single batman which most officers had. They were a cook, a personal 'batman', and a cleaner, whom they called a 'sweeper'. The only other brick building was the Company Headquarters where I had my office, and a court for use when a visiting magistrate came round to try alleged delinquents. I was the only white and so it was a bit on the lonely side, but occasionally other officers visited me on their way through to other similar camps or villages, and they stayed with me.

My main duty there was to keep law and order in an area of several thousand square miles. It sounded a lot but there was really not much there apart from desert and scrub, and a few villages even smaller than Villabruzzi. There had been many instances of raids on neighbouring villages and settlements by tribes, known as the Shifta, from the neighbouring country of Ethiopia – who pillaged, raped and mutilated many of the inhabitants. The usual trick was that when there was knowledge of an impending raid, and it was amazing how quickly the news came through even without mobile telephones, the Gendarmerie surrounded a water-hole which the Shifta would require for their camels and themselves, and then refuse them water until they handed over their weapons. This usually did the trick. I understood later that the weapons which the Gendarmerie took were sent back to base and eventually sent to the Ethiopian King, Haile Selaisse, to help him maintain law and order. However it appears that the King then sold them to the Shifta tribes which gave him a source of income, and so in a sense the weapons were continually recycled.

This constant patrolling had its benefits for me. Our only transport was a 2-ton Chevrolet truck, and although I had a driver I usually drove it myself. From time to time I arranged to go out very early in the morning, when the wild game were still roaming, and it was like a modern trip in the game reserves in Zimbabwe or South Africa, which we have since visited. Of course I had no camera but I did have a rifle, an army 303 calibre. I used to stand on the back of the lorry to give me the advantage of seeing further, and when game came into sight I ordered my driver to pursue them. Then from the back of the lorry I could pick off whatever game I could manage to hit.

I usually felled them with one round, but I do recall one occasion when I hit an Oryx in the flank. It continued to run with this great hole in its side. I quickly gave it a coup de grace, but I can still see it and it still worries me, although to go big-game hunting in those days was a normal sporting practice and the locals were unable to understand my concern. I ordered my men to remove the horns and the front of the skull to which they were attached, and then I put them away ready for when I would eventually return home. All this had to be done at first light because as soon as the sun was up the wild life took cover. These horns, and others, still grace our hall. It was a very different era then. We fairly recently came back from a cruise carrying a turtle which we had bought in Casablanca as a lampshade. When we arrived in Tilbury the customs officer, very apologetically, told us that it was 'protected species' and confiscated it. I wonder what he would have said about oryx horns! A little later I received the credit card bill for the lamp shade I never had!

One day we were driving past a tributary of the Juba River when the water was disturbed by a hippopotamus. I got out of the Chevrolet. The hippo was perfectly still, with just the top if its head and eyes above the water. Before I could take aim my sergeant-major told me that the hide was so thick that the only way of killing it was to hit it with one clean shot in the eye or the ear. I did that and my accuracy paid off again. What troubled me, though, was that the hippo immediately sank.

I was told not to worry: I was advised that in two hours it would rise to the surface. We waited and in two hours it did just that – except it came up on the other side of the river, which at this point was about thirty feet wide. I told one of the men to swim out to attach a rope to it so that we could pull it across and somehow land it. He told me rather nervously that there were crocodiles in the river. I asked him what he feared more – the crocodiles or me. He jumped in. I held my breath, but he got across and attached the rope. I held my breath again when he swam back, but the crocodiles must have been afraid of me as well because they held off. But when I look back on it now I am utterly and completely horrified with myself! How times have changed!

When we got the hippo to our side the problem was how to land it. We had a two-ton winch, to be used if the Chevrolet got stuck, and we attached that to the hippo, but as it was being pulled up the chain broke. This led me to the conclusion that the hippo weighed more than two tons. We then attached the rope to the back of the lorry, and with the effort of the lorry and the matched effort of my men we gradually managed to pull it on to the bank.

I then gave instructions for some strips of the hide to be cut so that I could use them as riding crops, and I used one of those for many years back in England. Talk about 'bullshit', I think that to have a hippo-hide riding crop which you had shot yourself really gave you the accolade. They cut out, as well, some of the larger teeth, which I still have. Today the only shooting you do is with a camera.

We moved away a bit whilst we sorted things out, as the hippo was beginning to smell – the temperatures were, as one might say, 'tropical'. Before you could say knife there were, coming from nowhere, vultures circling above and so we moved a little further away again. Literally within minutes these vultures, and their friends, had eaten the whole of the carcase, just leaving a pile of bones behind.

This side of things was all very well. I could handle hippos, oryx and large buck as well as wild pigs – I have the teeth of one of those somewhere too – but in my own bungalow one of the main problems was to keep on top of the wild life that really worried me then and worries me now – creepy crawlies. One day I opened a kitchen cupboard and saw that is was full of cockroaches. I loathed, and still loathe, them. I got my three servants to clear every corner in the bungalow to make sure we were rid of them. I had not realised, even after being in Egypt and other parts of Kenya and Somalia, that there should be so many of them and so persistent. I always tell my wife, who does not share this fear, that if she looks after the odd wood louse or beetle in the garden or even in the house, I will look after the lions and tigers, the really big stuff. So far it has worked out very well.

Very occasionally brother officers were passing through and so we had a party. If we were lucky the visitors might be in pairs or even threes, and so we could really celebrate. They were all English-speaking occasions, of course, which was a refreshing change from Swahili. Occasionally there would be a visiting magistrate calling at the Headquarters – an army major – called to try local cases as one would in a magistrates' court. It was very similar to the Mogadishu experience save that the interpreter was even worse, and we had to rely on Swahili pretty well from start to finish. Again I was the prosecutor and there were no defending advocates, which made my task easier. There were, so far as I recall, no acquittals. But the visitor would be my guest at my bungalow as well, so I had some company from time to time.

Life went on with this routine, with early morning hunting parties, very occasional visitors, looking out for marauding tribes, and keeping the village in working order. From time to time I inspected my troops' married quarters. They consisted of round mud huts with straw roofs, the floor being the earth, and with their few personal belongings arranged within. The men and their wives stood stiffly to attention as I inspected. What always amazed me, and still does, is that despite the conditions the huts were immaculate, tidy and clean, and the men were always smart in their uniforms and the wives in their local dress, which was one very colourful cloth wrapped round so as to give complete modesty, comfort, and colour. The men's uniforms were khaki-drill, a 'kula na kelemba' headdress (a cap without a peak held on with a turban), always clean and pressed.

Then one day there was a knock on my front door and to my surprise it was the Colonel – the full colonel. He was in command not only of the Gendarmerie but also of all troops in the area. I went to the door to greet him. We had got to know each other quite well in Mogadishu and I naturally assumed that he was passing through on his way to somewhere else – there was really nothing for him in Villabruzzi. He looked rather serious and he had a piece of paper in his hand.

His opening words were:- 'I am sorry, I have some rather bad news for you. Here is a telegram to say that your father has died'. He meant well, and if news like that is to be broken one might as well do it that way as any other. He handed me the piece of paper. It was a telegram. It read 'Please break news Captain Neville Goldrein father died today. Doctor requests immediate compassionate posting England'. The colonel continued, 'Is there anything else I can do? I shall arrange the posting to the U.K.'. I replied that there was nothing more and that I would wait to hear from him. He bade me farewell and I saluted. There was no such thing as counselling in those days and, quite frankly, I think generally it is a load of nonsense these days. There was such a thing as the British stiff upper lip, and I still think that is a better answer than counselling.

A message had come at the same time that there was a telephone call for me at Headquarters from Captain Ted Percival, my old friend from Mogadishu. In a daze I jumped in my Chev and drove across. Telephoning was not so quick in those days but I was through in under half an hour. I had still not properly absorbed the terrible news. When Ted came on it transpired that he did not know if the colonel had reached me, and as my closest friend he wanted to break the news to me himself. I thanked him and put the 'phone down. News travels very quickly and I heard one of my sergeants say to one of the men that my father had died.

That seemed to be a confirmation – I had now heard it from the lips of three people. The stiff upper lip remained. It was a point of honour then – and I still think it is better that way – to keep one's grief to oneself, if one can do it. I went back to my bungalow, dismissed the staff for the afternoon, locked the door, went to my bedroom – and wept. Tears still come to my eyes even now when I think of it. When I recovered I recited 'kaddish', the Jewish mourning prayer, in Hebrew. I did that twice a day for a month. It was not that I thought that the Almighty would intervene – indeed my father had been such a good man that I felt that intervention was completely unnecessary – but I said it out of respect for a very beloved father. And on the anniversary of his death, as is a Jewish custom, I still recite the same prayer.

I tried to carry on normally and by concentrating on my work I could bear the pain a little more easily. I was awaiting details of the posting to England, and had no idea of what the future had in hand. One of the worst parts was the complete lack of information other than the telegram. I had known that my father was due to have an operation for a duodenal ulcer – something that I understand just does not happen these days as there are many better means of treatment – but it never occurred to me that it could be fatal or even dangerous. It transpired later that three days after the operation – he had, as was the custom in those days, been kept in bed with little movement, compared with today when they are up as soon as possible to prevent this happening – he developed a pulmonary embolism and just had time to say to my mother, who was at his bedside, 'Kiss me', and then he died.

And so I waited. It is hard to recall how long it was but with communications as they were, or were not, in those days, it must have been a good month before I received instructions to go back to Mogadishu for the first stage of my journey home. I had to get from Villabruzzi to Mogadishu, and so I drove, not trusting my driver. As we left I was asked by my cook if I could give a lift to him and his wife, so I put them in the back of the open truck and drove off. To be in the back, with all the dust and sand, was certainly unpleasant and people travelling there, black or white, ended up sand-coloured and sand-covered. Nowadays I would have squeezed them with me in front but in those days that would have been unheard-of. My driver was in the back as well.

As I drove along I saw some people – locals – walking along the mud road, and by way of arrogant fun I drove at them and then swerved, and fortunately missed them. They took it well and waved. Then there was a sudden banging on the roof to the cab, and my driver shouted down that I should stop urgently as 'The cook's wife is dead sir'! That was in Swahili but the meaning was abundantly clear. I stopped.

There was the cook's wife lying in the road about one hundred yards behind, but as I ran up to her I could, to my relief, detect movement. Then even without help she managed to get up. It transpired that she had been sitting on the tailboard and when I swerved she had fallen off. I had not given any thought to the people travelling in the back. She could indeed have been badly hurt. Once I saw that she was alright I told them all that they had to sit well within the truck before I drove off.

To let some air in, as this really was tropical heat being a matter of a few miles from the Equator, I kept the windscreen propped open. Suddenly the cab was filled with locusts, and although I closed the windscreen as quickly as I could they still filled the cab and continued to come in through the side windows. I was covered in them. I realised then what the Eighth Plague was about. I got the passengers to clear the cab of as many locusts as they could, closed the windows and windscreen, and drove off. Those in the back must have had it pretty rough until we cleared the locust cloud, and it was a cloud. They left absolutely nothing behind – they nearly did not even leave me behind!

When we got to Mogadishu I told my driver to take the trusty Chev back and I went to the Headquarters mess - the Duke of Aosta's Palace. I was given a temporary job, whilst awaiting further orders, being in charge of the Claims Commission, whose task was to deal with unused and unwanted tanks, trucks, firearms and the rest and to try to see that they were accounted for.

Then some weeks later the order came through. I was to get back to Nairobi for the start of my journey home. This was in the 'Somali Mail', an old bus which plied between Mogadishu and Nairobi – run and driven by Rihani - and took five days, with us sleeping out next to fires to keep off the jackals in the same way as when we had come. I remember little of the journey save that it was very boring and seemed to be endless. I had no brother-officers to keep me company.

Another problem – not really a problem but a nuisance – was that I had been promoted to the rank of captain when I was in Villabruzzi, but the system was that when one moved to another job he reverted to his 'War Substantive Rank', so I was back to being a lieutenant.

Nairobi, which, by comparison with what I had lived through for many months, was civilization and comfort, and being some 7,000 feet high, it is a cooler city with a lovely climate. The first stage was to get to Cairo, and so after a few days I boarded a Lockheed Lodestar of RAF Transport Command to cover the first leg. Nowadays, of course, Nairobi to London is one hop and pretty quick at that. But the Lodestar was big by the standards of the day, with over thirty passengers. My heavy tin trunk had to go by sea and arrived home some months later. I took with me only the essentials – including the horns of the animals I had shot on safari, rolled up in my holdall/sleeping bag.

I saw, flying below us, a flying boat, doing more or less the same journey, and though the flying boats were slow, they were, so I was told, very comfortable. Apparently you could wander about, look out of the open windows, and relax. They did not fly very high or very fast – about a hundred miles an hour. In any case in our 'faster' aeroplane we could not get to Cairo in one hop and we got as far as Khartoum the first day. There we alighted and went to reasonably adequate accommodation for the night. I wanted to go out and look at the town but there was nobody to accompany me. One officer on the flight whom I had approached was not interested, and to be on my own, in a strange Sudanese City at night was, I thought, foolhardy, and so I went to bed.

The next morning we boarded the same aircraft and by teatime we were in Cairo - a whole day for a journey which today might take a couple of hours. From the airport a truck took me and others to the Abbassiya Barracks where I was given a room and messing facilities – that does not mean that I messed but that there was the officers' mess where

I could eat and relax. I was there for only a few days but I did not want to move far away in case there was a sudden notice regarding my departure. In addition I was on my own, everybody else was in transit, and there was no company of any kind.

Then suddenly the next stage had arrived. I was notified that the following day at 3 a.m. I would be travelling to London in an Avro York of R.A.F. Transport Command. It was the civilian version of the Lancaster bomber, very large by the standards of those days – it had four engines and the military version could take a load of ten tons of bombs. The transport version could take over forty passengers, and there were two toilets. Better than the facilities of today! The aircraft was not pressurised and the height at which we flew was generally about 9,000 feet, as, indeed, the flight report states, but on one occasion we got up to about 20,000 feet to avoid bad weather and the air was pretty thin. So we had to take the oxygen masks from above our heads – the type of thing that is only used in emergencies these days – and hold it over our noses and mouths. The chap sitting next to me, an 'other rank' (in other words, not an officer) only had a tube – the mask part had disappeared, and he could not be bothered to use it. I suddenly noticed that he passed out, and quickly stuck the tube in his mouth, and round he came. I did not ask him but ordered him to keep the tube there until it was safe to remove it. Otherwise I suppose he could have died.

I still have the flight report, which was, in those days, handwritten by the pilot and handed round. We were not only flying at such a height, but at the enormous speed of 201 mph. It was something to tell my friends. However despite the size of the aircraft which had taken off from Cairo at about three o'clock in the morning, we had to stop in Malta at about 9 o'clock to refuel. Once on the ground I was escorted to the officers' mess for breakfast, and then back to the aircraft at about ten o'clock to continue the journey to the RAF aerodrome at Swindon. It had taken fifteen hours which these days would take you from London to Tokyo.

Once off the aircraft I was given a truck to take me to the railway station, armed with a rail travel warrant to London. There was a little café or snack place on the platform. It was February and very very cold, particularly by comparison with the temperatures to which I had become accustomed. I went into the little bar to ask for a double whisky, which I knocked back in one gulp like a vodka. The lady behind the counter looked in wonder at this young officer drinking so much so quickly, particularly when I ordered a second one. It did warm me up but it cost me about a week's pay. Then the train came and I was nearly at the end of my journey home.

-oOo--

Chapter 8
Back In Blighty

The arrangement was that I should travel to London to meet my Mother at the Howard Hotel which belonged to my Uncle Charles and where mother was staying to be with the family after my Father's death. My brother had been released from the army to resume his studies at Cambridge and so she would have been alone. At the Howard she was with family – my Uncle and Aunt Eva, (her brother-in-law and sister), and various other family members.

My train arrived and off I got with my kit – the rolled-up camp-bed\holdall - with my bits and pieces and wearing my slouch hat, all looking very much from the Empire. I took a taxi to the Howard and was met by the concierge, whom I knew of old, very warmly. As my luggage was brought in to the foyer of the hotel my holdall came apart revealing my most valuable possessions – the horns of the animals I had shot in Somalia. I had not realised that horns are not just horns set in bone, but that they were originally held in place by various bodily fluids and some more solid substances. As they fell out the horns came off the bones leaving behind oozing splurge with a very strong, and not 'Howard Hotel-like', odour. The staff quickly put them on one side and then took them to the cellar so that I could go in to see my mother. She was in the hotel lounge with the family, and there was I, the 'glamorous' young officer just retuned from the other end of the world, as it almost was in those days, and we hugged. Mother wept. I had, as I have said, been brought up to the culture of the stiff upper lip, and I managed to keep it that way. Men did not cry in those days, whatever the circumstances.

To me it was wonderful in one sense to be back to civilization, family, and lovely surroundings. The great thing was that, had I retuned home normally, and not in such tragic circumstances, I would not have seen Dad at the Howard anyway as he would have been in Liverpool at his office. And so whilst we were in London I was able in a sense to suppress the thoughts of his death, and to comfort Mum as best I could. Dad was not there, but he would not have been there anyway.

Then the time came for us to return to Liverpool. Just before I went abroad my parents had bought a house in Childwall, a Liverpool suburb, which I had only seen for a moment to look at it before the actual purchase, but where I had never lived. We had been in a rented house in Broadgreen when I left. Not having lived there I had never known my father there and so I had no memories of him there. That made the loss easier to bear. I missed him in my heart and mind - I still do – but not physically. We had been together when I had been on vacation from Cambridge and on leave from the army, but that had been at the house in Broadgreen and had we still lived there I would have seen him in every corner. In the new house I was to some extent protected from this sense of physical loss.

Back home I had few friends in Liverpool, but there were cousins in the Wirral and some friends of my parents. But so far as I was concerned, to be home, on leave, was wonderful relaxation, with the knowledge that by being with Mum the whole time I could keep her mind partially off her terrible loss.

So I waited for the Army to tell me where to go and what to do. Typically of the Army, I heard nothing for what seemed ages but which must have been a month, when suddenly there was a letter to say that I had been posted to be on the staff of the Transit Camp at a place called Kirkby, and to report that very day. One wonders how we won the war.

I put my bits and pieces together, realising that I could always get home to pick up anything I had forgotten, but I knew nothing of Kirkby. I knew that there was a West Kirby in the Wirral, on the other side of the River Mersey, and assumed that it must be there, and so telephoned a taxi. The driver told me that there was indeed a place called Kirkby – with a 'k' in it - being a fairly new industrial suburb of Liverpool which was called, not politically incorrectly in those days, 'working-class'. One could almost be drummed out of the brownies for saying things like that today.

At Kirkby there was a large transit camp where troops on leave from India and the Far East came to be processed and sent home, and then on their return at the end of their leave we had to ensure that they were properly embarked on the right ship at the right time. There was an adjutant called 'Ticky' Leech who never had a cigarette out of his mouth – he coughed incessantly and told me that the cough was from the smoking which was healthy and helped him to clear his lungs – and I was to help in his office with the ever-increasing numbers passing through the camp under the title of Assistant Adjutant.

There was no system at all, and I wonder now how anyone ever got home or ever got back. Perhaps they never arrived. And so, as I was there, I thought that I might as well work out a system, and Ticky Leech had no objection so long as he was not too involved. I worked out a register so that, after a comparatively short time, I could be asked the name of any officer or other rank and advise as to all details, whereabouts, dates of return and so on. There were no computers in those days – this was all on paper and with a card index.

There was a fairly small staff, and two of the officers had served in the 1914-1918 War. They must have been in their forties and seemed ancient to me, but we got on well except for one dark occasion. We were in the Officers' Mess having lunch and were discussing the black market. This was still a real problem as so many things were in short supply. I stated my views. I have forgotten precisely what I said but it was in no way offensive. Then Fred Rowley, one of the 'elderly' subalterns, said 'I would take that from a gentile but not from a bloody Jew'! This was the first and only anti-Semitism I had met in the army, and after a six-year war predominately against the Germans and the horrors of the concentration camps, the news of which was now coming through in great detail, I was horrified. This was what we had fought against, and here was a British Officer behaving like – a Nazi.

I excused myself to the Colonel, got up and walked out to the ante-room – the equivalent of the lounge. The colonel immediately followed me and apologised, and said that he would deal with the matter. He was followed by all the others and in front of them all Fred Rowley apologised. I accepted his apology but I still remain horrified that such a remark was made.

During this time I managed to arrange to spend three weeks at an Army College – this was to teach us to be civilians and to give us an insight into the work which we would be doing. My career was to be the Law. There was no Law training at Army College but that did not put them, or me, off.

I went to Dalkeith, near Edinburgh, to Newbattle Abbey, the seat of the Earls of Dalkeith. There was no academic work for me to do so I spent the three weeks looking round Edinburgh, always a beautiful city, visiting the Officers' Club, and hiring a hack and horse-riding in King's Park – now known as Queen's Park. I was riding with two colleagues one day when a large black limousine stopped and some very high-ranking army officers got out and went for a walk. I rode nearer to them and realised that I was alongside His Majesty King George VI. I, from the height of my horse, looked down on His Majesty, saluted smartly – which he returned – and cantered off.

Then the time came to return to Huyton and the routine continued. Most week-ends I borrowed an army 15 cwt (hunderedweight) truck to get home – it was only four or five miles away. (I will never know why we gave up that pure logic of 16 ounces to the pound, 14 pounds to the stone, 112 pounds to the hundredweight and 2240 pounds to the ton in favour of the metric system). On a Sunday afternoon on 2nd August 1947 I was at home when the telephone rang. My mother took the call. I was next to her and I could hear the conversation. I heard a female voice ask if this was the home of Dr Goldrein. My mother explained that the name was Goldrein, but there was no doctor in the family. The voice said that she understood that Dr Goldrein was the brother of a Mrs Share in Newcastle-upon-Tyne. My mother explained that unfortunately her husband had died and that he had no relatives in Newcastle. The voice said that she had clearly made a mistake and wished to hang up, being most apologetic for disturbing us.

My mother insisted – she was curious. The voice explained that her name was Sonia Sumner, that she was a newly-qualified doctor and had her first 'house job' at the Liverpool Heart Hospital, and that her neighbour in Newcastle, Mrs Share, had suggested that she should ring Mrs Share's brother, Dr Goodman who practised in Liverpool, so that she would have a contact in Liverpool when she arrived. By pure coincidence Dr Goodman was my Mother's doctor. The problem was that the caller had muddled the two names – Goodman and Goldrein. The reason was that at about the same time a friend of my brother Eric, Arthur Taylor, whom he had met at Cambridge and with whom he had remained in touch, had a brother, Peter, who later became the Lord Chief Justice of England. I found out later that Peter used to play the piano with this girl, and had suggested that she should ring Eric Goldrein when she got to Liverpool, but she had hastily replied that – as was the case in those days - she would not ring a house where there were boys. Girls were very much more reticent then.

My mother still insisted – her curiosity remained - and ascertained that the girl was on her own, new to Liverpool and said that we would come to the Hospital to pick her up so that she could come to us for tea. The girl, most embarrassed, tried to refuse but my mother was adamant. My mother was clearly curious too, and I wonder if she thought that I, new to Liverpool, had few friends and this may have been an opportunity to meet somebody new.

We got into the car – a Ford Prefect – and I drove, my mother being a non-driver. We approached the hospital and, standing on the steps, was a dark haired girl in a green suit, yellow blouse, brown shoes, big brown eyes – obviously our target. I exclaimed enthusiastically, 'Not bad!'. We drew up, and she was as good close-up as she had been in the distance. I invited her into the car – 'hop in' - and off we went and took her home. I gathered later that she was a little suspicious of me because I had a moustache and suede shoes, both signs of a reprobate! As far as I was concerned she was, and has always remained, the loveliest girl I had ever met, her voice was right, everything about her fitted in to my ideal woman.

When we got home I invited her into the garden and got out two deck-chairs. No sooner had we sat down than it started to rain, and we had to go in. I was very worried in case I had made a fool of myself – although she later made it abundantly clear that that was not the case. As the afternoon wore on my conviction that she was 100% right was confirmed moment by moment. In the evening I ran her back to the hospital, formally said good-night and arranged to meet her again on, I think, the following Tuesday evening, the first time she would be free.

I was in a turmoil of excitement and I clearly recall that I did not sleep properly for four or five nights, from sheer excitement. I would have proposed then but I was still in the army, I had no job and no qualifications, and I feared that I would have frightened her off. Anyway I was sure that no girl would accept a proposal after the first meeting!

On the Tuesday I took her to a dance at the Tower Ballroom in New Brighton, in the Wirral. We danced and chatted and all my thoughts were confirmed. That was the first evening, too, when I had worn a civilian suit, as was allowed by then. I found that she did not drink alcohol, not out of conviction but because it upset her tummy. I saw her back to the hospital. Again there was a fairly formal 'good-night' and we arranged to meet again.

I think the next meeting was for tea at the Lyceum Café in Bold Street Liverpool. She had an afternoon off. I had to collect some troops from the docks, and then I would be free as well. My work took a little longer than I had anticipated but when I got to the cafe I was relieved to see her just arriving. Later I found that she had been there on time but, quite rightly, did not wish to sit there waiting for me in case I did not turn up or was very late, and so went for a walk round and then returned. We had tea. We chatted, and I had no doubt that she was for me. From the moment I set eyes on her there has never been another woman in my life.

My time now came to be 'demobbed' – demobilized for those who forget the jargon of the time. I went up to York, with the Army's usual efficiency of arranging for the procedure to take place at their regimental depot – I was in the East Yorkshire Regiment although I had never served with them - rather than at the local depot round the corner. On arrival I was taken, apart from completing forms in probably triplicate, to receive a suit, shirt, tie, trilby hat, mackintosh, socks and shoes, which were then placed in a brown box which had been designed to fit the 'trousseau', and off home I went – a civilian!

--oOo--

Chapter 9
A Civilian At Last

I then had to start serious work for my future career, and with Sonia in the offing that was a very serious matter. I could have gone to Guildford near London for a residential course to study for the Solicitors' exams, but I had been away from home for four years and preferred to adopt the far more difficult option of doing the work from home by correspondence course. The really important reason for this, though, was that Sonia, whom I hardly knew but liked so much, was in Liverpool and not in Guildford.

During the day I worked, as Sonia was working in the hospital, and sometimes in the evenings too. The course was usually a little over two years, and included one exam on Bookkeeping and Trust Accounts, which had a 50% failure rate, and the other was the Final which had a similar failure rate.

In the odd spare evenings and at week-ends Sonia and I met, went out, talked, went to parties and telephoned each other, but I still did not say how I felt in case my being too precipitate would put her off. On the other hand if I delayed it somebody else might get in and I would lose my chance. After three or, at most, four weeks, and in case she should meet anyone else, I felt that the die had to be cast. We had been out for the evening and were sitting the car outside the Hospital. We chatted for a few minutes, she was about to get out, when I took my courage into both hands and said 'Sonia, I love you and I want to marry you'. She was quite astonished but, I was relieved to see, not displeased. She said that she had been at school, university, a trainee doctor, and at last she had her freedom and although she liked me very much she did not know if she wished to be committed and tied up again so soon. We said good-night and I gave her a slight peck on the cheek. She did not object.

I went on 'pressing my suit' daily and after about six seeks – it seemed like years – she said she loved me too and agreed to accept the proposal. I was in seventh heaven, and again I could not sleep for several nights. We decided not to make it public before we told the families. My mother was delighted, and Sonia's mother came for a day or two ostensibly to see Sonia but really the idea was for her to meet me. I remember that the two of us, our mothers and Eric had dinner at the Adelphi Hotel. As Sonia took her Mum to her room after dinner she said, 'By the way, do you like Neville, because he wants to marry me?'. She left her mother to her thoughts – and no doubt to a sleepless night – but fortunately she approved. To this day – over sixty years later - I still get a thrill when I recall those days – and so does Sonia.

The next thing was for us, with my mother and brother Eric, to visit Newcastle-on-Tyne to meet Sonia's father and family. We were very warmly received and immediately made to feel at home. I made one mistake. One of Sonia's cousins was called Effie (Ephraim) Anderson, a micro-biologist and very clever and who was later appointed C.B.E. for his services to research. He was also on the face of it a warm and friendly personality and he asked me out for a beer at the local. I am not a great pub-goer, but I felt that it was right to do the thing that this senior cousin had suggested I should do and off we went. What I did not realise was that Effie, who was so warm towards me, was in fact the black sheep of the family which disapproved of pubs anyway! Fortunately they forgave me.

Each side approved of the other, save that we all knew that there was a wait of some two years before I qualified, and I was not prepared to marry before then as that would have meant being dependent on my mother or on Sonia's minute salary, at that time under £2 per week – rather more in those days than today but by no means enough to live on! I knew I wanted to marry Sonia and that was no problem, and it was no problem for Sonia either as she knew I loved her. I cannot blame her parents, though, for being concerned as a young man can change his mind in such a long period. We went back to Newcastle at the end of the year for a formal engagement party. The families met and many friends came to join in. I was on Cloud Nine.

Then back to the real world and work. Sonia was wonderful. She would come over in the evenings after her work and just sit and read in the room where I was working. I worked all day in the office where I was articled and every evening I worked at home apart from Thursday and weekends. As I worked she sat and read and never complained. I had one main objective, and that was to reduce the two years plus to 18 months, after which time it was possible to take the Final exams but not recommended as it meant a considerable cram of work.

As an Articled Clerk – these days they are called Trainee Solicitors – we were not paid. Indeed I paid my principals for allowing me to be articled, and it cost me the whole of my War Gratuity, paid to demobbed ex-servicemen, which was over £400, a fortune in those days. And so every day, not only receiving no pay, but paying for the privilege, I worked a full day in the office, learning the 'trade' and being let loose on clients, sitting with counsel in court, preparing conveyances, wills, the lot. And it had to be right because if I got it wrong my firm could be sued for negligence and my future would have been ruined.

I took the Book-keeping Exam in the Spring and to my amazement I passed, although then, as now, accounts have never been my strongest point, to put it at its highest. The failure rate was just over 50% so how I passed I shall never know. Then I took my Finals in June of 1949 where the failure rate was similar. I was sure that I had failed and in desperation arranged to go on a residential course at Guildford for the next term to make sure that I would pass second time round. I started to work again, as I had before, day in and day out. Sonia showed her usual wonderful patience.

And then one morning I got in to the office and Ted Hand, the cashier, said 'Congratulations!'. I enquired as to what I had done to deserve congratulations, and he told me that he had been told by a representative from the Law Stationers that I had passed. My reply was 'Rubbish, I did appallingly and there is no chance'. He insisted. I did not believe him. I telephoned the Law Stationers and they confirmed it. I still did not believe them and so I telephoned the Law Society itself and to my amazement they confirmed it too. I was in a dream. The impossible had happened – particularly when I discovered later that there had been a failure rate of 52%.

That meant that we could get married! But first, Sonia was entitled to know before anyone. So I telephoned the surgery – she was an assistant doctor in private practice at this time – and spoke to Mrs Grant, the caretaker who looked after the surgery, and asked her to tell Dr Sumner – Sonia - that Dr Brown (her employer) wanted to see her and she should not leave until he arrived. In the meantime I bought the biggest bunch of flowers I could afford and dashed off in the car to the surgery. There she was standing waiting for Dr Brown, I had the flowers concealed behind my back, but she could not understand what I was doing there. Then I produced the flowers, told her that I had passed and that we would get married. We threw ourselves into each other's arms, and Mrs Grant burst into tears. I then suggested that we should go out to celebrate if only by having a cup of coffee somewhere. But Sonia told me that we had to wait until Dr Brown came and so we waited. Suddenly I realised that I was the Dr Brown! Off we went able at last to start our lives together.

--oOo--

CHAPTER 10
The Dream becomes Real

B efore marrying, there still remained one problem – I had to make a living. By this time Sonia was working as an assistant doctor in general practice which kept her busy, was excellent training, and she was paid what was then, but certainly not now, reasonable remuneration. Even had I been new-fashioned enough to be kept by my wife, she could hardly, with the best will in the world, have kept us in the manner to which we wished to be accustomed.

The firm to which I was articled did not immediately offer me a job, and I had the feeling that this was not because of ill-will, but that they took it for granted that I would stay on when my articles expired, which was a few weeks from the announcement of the results. I have never been prepared to be taken for granted, and so I started to look round. One has to work out the changing values of money, and at that time the offer I had from one firm of £300 per annum was not too bad - one must remember that even a County Court Judge, the equivalent of a Circuit judge today, was only paid about £2000 per annum, and that was considered very generous indeed.

So after receiving that and similar offers, which confirmed to me that that was about the going rate, I mentioned to my principals that I had been offered a job and would be leaving on the expiration of my articles. This took them completely by surprise and I am pleased, looking back, that I managed, despite my inexperience, to play them as I did. They retired to consult and asked me what I had been offered. I replied that it would not be fair to my future employers to give them such a detail as it could be considered a breach of confidence. They retired again. Shortly afterwards they returned and offered me £600 per annum, a very generous offer to a newly-qualified assistant solicitor at that time. I told them that I would let them know the next day, although clearly, so far as I was concerned, it was an offer too good to be missed. In addition I had been quite happy there in my articles, I knew the office and the people, and was really taking no risks by accepting – and so I did.

That problem solved we set about the wedding – whom to ask, the numbers, the location of the ceremony, the reception, the dress, the lot. I was not keen on the synagogue which Sonia and her family normally attended in Newcastle, and preferred another synagogue in Jesmond which we had visited on one occasion just to see what it was like. It struck me as much more friendly and warm and the Reverend Drukker, who was in charge, was a delightful man. I think I had a tremendous impertinence to suggest that Sonia's parents should have the wedding in a synagogue other than their own, if not only because of the embarrassment it could cause them but because it might not have been their choice. They not only did not complain but agreed willingly and throughout I could not fault their attitude towards me – nor could I ever thereafter. Sonia agreed with my choice, we both liked the Rev. Drukker, who would marry us, and so all was set fair for the wedding to take place on October 30th 1949, a little more than two years after we had met.

Then there was another problem – but a very pleasant one: Where to honeymoon? My principals had had a holiday not long before in a place, little heard of, called Majorca. They had been most impressed by it and they could give us a lot of information about it. One must remember that in those days there were few travel agents, not a lot of foreign travel, being so soon post-war, and detailed advice such as they gave was of tremendous importance. And so I went to Thos. Cook's office and enquired about Majorca. The assistant asked, 'Where is that?'. I turned the globe on his office counter and pointed to it. He said 'But that is Mallorca, not Majorca'. I explained that this was because the Spanish could not spell properly but that they really were one and the same place. And so we booked for as long a honeymoon as we could afford, or rather more than we could really afford – about eight days.

Then we had to find somewhere to live. One evening, when we knew we could at last get married, Sonia had to visit a patient in a place called Blundellsands, a fair way from the surgery in Bootle where Sonia worked, but the practice was wide-spread. We drove up to a large detached house on the very edge of the green belt and about a quarter of a mile from the sea. I sat outside in the car and Sonia went in to see the patient, who was the maid. A few minutes later the owner of the house, a Miss Williams, came out and asked me if I would like to come in rather than wait outside. In I went, and was offered, and accepted, a whiskey and a cigarette from a beautiful silver cigarette box. I smoked in those days, as most people did.

Miss Williams and her family remained friends for years, but the thing that she really achieved was that she introduced us to Blundellsands. As we drove away we both thought that it would be a delightful place to live, and not too far from Dr Brown's practice where Sonia worked. And as we looked round in the days to come I mentioned it to Ted Hand, the cashier in the office, and he suggested that we should find a plot of land in the area and build a new house on it. We thought this well beyond our means, anticipating that we would be lucky if we could manage a small three-bedroom semi-detached.

We did not know Merseyside – or Lancashire – very well, and Blundellsands was new to us. It derives its name from the Blundell family, who came to Crosby, in which Blundellsands is situated, in 1115, and have lived there ever since. They were, and still are, the major landowners in the area and still live very nearby.

So we looked round and found three plots, all quite near to Miss Williams, and owned by the building firm of Costains. We went to their office and told them that we particularly liked one of the plots. We were told that there was a government limit of 1500 superficial feet to any new house constructed, and that the cost could not exceed £2 per foot. That meant that the cost would be £3000. It was more than we had intended to spend but a purpose-built detached house was something which we had not expected to achieve and here was a chance. We thought it worth the struggle. There was a larger plot not far away and the cost of construction would have been the same, but there would have been an obligation on that plot to add another 500 square feet within ten years. That was an additional financial obligation which we were not prepared to face, although as it happened we could have achieved it. On the other hand the one we chose had sufficient advantages to leave us in no doubt. So the mortgage was arranged, the plans approved, and that left us only to find somewhere to live whilst it was being built.

The Blundells, being the landowners, owned our plot too, and we had to accept a 999-year lease. Fortunately because of government wartime restrictions the rent was limited to that payable for a piece of waste land, and so was ten shillings – fifty pence – per year. In due course we bought the freehold from the Blundells for £50, as it was costing them more than ten shillings a year to collect the rent.

We looked round for flats and found a small two room first floor flat in Waterloo, a little way down the line towards Liverpool, and started to pay the rent so that we could get organized.   Our landlady seemed to be alright. So all was prepared, and we got ready for the great day.

All was set up. My father's evening dress – white tie and tails – fitted me, and, of course, Sonia's wedding dress was kept a secret. All arrangements were made for the ceremony to be in Jesmond Synagogue and then the reception was to be at the Heaton Assembly Rooms in Newcastle. The family from London came up, the most important being my Uncle Charlie. As I has no father he had agreed to take my Father's place at the wedding ceremony. Also the evening before, instead of going out on the tiles and having a drunken bachelor party, he arranged a reception for family and close friends at the Royal Station Hotel, where they were staying. This kept us fairly sober, and meant that Sonia and I could be together. Then, very excited, this was followed by a fairly early night ready for the day for which we had waited for some two years.

The next day Sonia and I could not, of course, be together, but with the family there was plenty to do and to prepare. Eventually on went the white tie and tails, black topper and white carnation and off we went to Jesmond Synagogue. The wedding ceremony was at 6pm. I remember clearly standing under the Chuppah – the canopy – with my Uncle and Aunt and Mother next to me, waiting for Sonia to come in. Then I could hear the doors open and she had arrived. I looked round smiling to see Sonia looking gorgeous on the arm of her father, also in full evening dress. As I looked round my Uncle turned to me and said 'Take it seriously!' - which was an indication that the family regarded me as rather a playboy and that this was all part of the fun. To me it was very very serious, and I still remember Sonia coming in and standing next to me for the ceremony. To this day I am pleased I turned round as she came in.

Then it was over, we were told that we were man and wife, and I gave Sonia a gentle kiss on the cheek – I felt, and she felt, that a kiss on the lips was too personal to be done in public, but that kiss on the cheek remains in my memory as yesterday.

We were then taken in the wedding car to the reception. Afterwards Sonia told me that she expected me to say something about the seriousness of the wedding, and that at last we were on our own, married. Instead I said ' I'm looking forward to the party'! This was not that I was casual about being a newly-wed, but the whole thing was a culmination of so many hopes, and I was so happy that I was just revelling in every moment of it.

The next thing was the photographs – lots of them as always, standing, sitting, with family and without. Whilst the photographers were setting it up I was so happy with every moment that I started to dance a 'kazatski', a Russian dance which I had seen and where you get right down and throw your feet forwards. I managed it without a fault with applause from the family before the next picture was taken.

The reception was a dinner as it was a Sunday evening and the local bye-laws at the time did not allow music or dancing. The meal was, so far as I recall, good, there were the speeches, and then we left the party to go to get changed and to return to say farewell – we had not told anybody where we were going for that night. So we left and went to change in another room, Sonia wearing a blue check suit and looking wonderful. She told me afterwards that she would have liked to have stayed in her wedding dress a little longer because, after all, it was a once-only event, but I did not realise that and wanted to be on my way with her away from the people – just the two of us.

Having changed we went back, waved good-night, and off we went to the Station Hotel. I recall a very nice bedroom with an open fire – because after all it was the end of October. Today I wonder how they could allow such things because of the fire danger, but that was the norm at that time. We ordered some sandwiches and felt very daring that the waiter should come into our bedroom and see us in our dressing gowns.

The next day we went to the station – which adjoined the hotel - to catch the Tyne-Tees Pullman train to London with first-class reserved seats. We could not really afford them but one only has a honeymoon once – or that was certainly the case so far as we were concerned. The train was very comfortable – a table for two facing each other, a lamp on the table, very personal service and food, and a bar alongside if we wanted a drink. The journey was about four hours – pulled, of course, by a steam engine in those days, and at London we had a limousine waiting for us to take us to the Hyde Park Hotel. As we drove off I must confess some satisfaction seeing Uncle Charlie and Auntie Eva trying to get a taxi whilst we went off in state.

We had arranged to go to the Hyde Park Hotel to have some tea before checking in for our flight, the first leg of the honeymoon. So far as I recall, we had to check in at Cromwell Road, to be taken by the airport bus to London Airport – at Northolt. The Hyde Park was, and still is, a lovely hotel and the tea was exactly right. The airport, which consisted of a number of wooden structures, could today be fitted into the tiniest corner of Heathrow. The aircraft was a Douglas Dakota, which carried about thirty passengers. In those days they were 'tail-wheel' aircraft – the aircraft was not level until it was in flight, and so you went up the gangway – there were no level approach corridors as there are today – and boarded at the rear of the aircraft, and then had to walk 'uphill' to our seats. We were only going to Paris but it was considered to be quite an adventure, we went at a speed of some 200 miles per hour, and the flight report read that we were flying at a height of 3,500 feet. The only problem was that it rather hurt Sonia's ears because there was no pressurisation.

We landed in Paris and there was a car waiting to take us to our hotel – not a five*+ by any means - but small and comfortable. The next day we took the train – after all, people at that time did not fly everywhere – to go to our first main stop, Barcelona. The train was very comfortable, I forget which class we used, and the frontier was crossed at Port Bou. There we had to get out and transfer to a Spanish train and all our luggage had to be checked by customs, which was done on the open platform. What we noticed particularly was that the customs officers were very off-hand and quite unfriendly to us – and we had just won the war – but treated other nationals in a far more friendly way. I think that perhaps they had been more pro-German than pro-British and still ticked that way. Fortunately we had no such problems after that. Then we boarded the Spanish train for the final leg to Barcelona. However we had one shock which was far worse than the unfriendliness of the Spaniards, and that was the rate of exchange. We had understood in England that there were 100 Spanish Pesetas to the Pound Sterling. However we were told that this was the summer rate, and that the winter rate, which had only just come in, was only 70 Pesetas to the Pound. That meant that our money was worth only 70% of what we had thought it was worth.

We journeyed through Spain to Barcelona. We stayed at a grand hotel and loved the city immediately. We visited Tibidabo, up on the hill where they had an amusement park and another hotel-cum-café, and then down again by the cable car. During the afternoon we were walking down the Ramblas – the wide thoroughfares which nowadays are mostly pedestrian - and sat in a hotel café for a cup of coffee and to discuss how we were going to manage with our 'wealth' reduced by some 30%. We were sitting opposite to a rather dark-skinned gentleman, whom we thought to be Spanish, and started to chat. He thought that we were pen-friends as we were clearly too young to be married! We told him we were on honeymoon. He had heard our chat about the rate of exchange and told us that his name was Shamdazani. He was an Indian businessman from London, and told us that he was returning to London the next day and that if we wanted to borrow any money to help us over he would gladly lend it to us. And so it was left that we would meet at Barcelona Airport the next morning, which tied up with our flight to Majorca. Imagine today arranging to meet somebody at an airport, with both parties flying to different places!

We decided that we would borrow ten pounds – a lot of money for us to repay in those days. We got to the airport and indeed there was Mr Shamdazani. He was as charming as ever, and gladly lent us the ten pounds. He pressed us to borrow more but we knew that we would have the problem of repayment. There was naturally no question of interest. He handed over the money and his visiting card so that we would know where to send it on our return home.

I offered him my card. He asked "What do I want that for? You need to know my address to know where to send the money, but I do not need to know your name and address". He refused to take my card, relying implicitly on the fact that I would repay. Naturally we sent a cheque immediately upon our return, but we cannot remember before or since such a warm genuine trusting gesture from a complete stranger. We kept in touch for many years by letter but unfortunately never met again. What a gentleman!

Then we flew to Majorca, hardly known in those days, and stayed in a district called 'Terreno', in the city of Palma - hence the name of our house, save that we misspelt it and our house is known as 'Torreno'. It was a lovely city, unspoilt by tourists at that time, and very picturesque. Then we went to the small village of Porto Cristo and on a day trip from there we went in a small boat to visit the Cuevas del Drach to see the caves with the stalagmites and stalactites – all very beautiful. The whole area was lovely.

One breakfast-time a gentleman with a smart cap, cravat and hacking jacket came in. He spoke like – and looked like - 'an English gentleman', as they did in those days, and said that he had heard that Sonia was a doctor. He was not a 'Mr.', but 'Colonel'. His wife, he said, was not very well, they did not trust foreigners, and he asked if Sonia would pop into their house nearby to check her out. Sonia did the necessary. Subsequently they took us out in their petrol-driven car – the only one in the area, the others all being driven by burning wood – to see some of the sights. He asked if we had ever been to Buckingham Palace, but at that time we had not and pleaded ignorance. He had had, he said, and we think it was probably true, tea with the Queen. A modest man.

The short honeymoon seemed even shorter and in due course we had to return home by train to Paris and by air to London Airport, Northolt, where the customs check was in a wooden shed. The aircraft could park very near and so it was only a short walk from there to the shed. What a different world! Then we returned up to Merseyside and went to our flat in Waterloo, a small first floor flat, and Sonia then went back to her work as a doctor with Dr David Brown, and I went to work with the firm in Birkenhead as had been arranged before we married.

In the meantime our flat was proving to be unsatisfactory because the landlady was far from helpful, and so we moved to another flat – a basement flat, which on the face of it was better. In the event it had its problems too. One Sunday afternoon we were entertaining guests when it started to pour with rain. This leaked in – or rather poured in – through one of the windows, which was at picture-rail height and which was hardly conducive to hospitable entertaining. Another 'inconvenience' was that the bath water was heated by a giant gas geyser which nearly exploded every time we lit it.

One night we were awakened by a rustling. Investigation showed that it was a mouse rooting round the remaining part of our wedding cake. I bravely said to my wife that I would deal with any intrusive lions or tigers, and that she could look after the small stuff, like mice and beetles. She played her part, as she always does, and the arrangement has remained to this day.

In the meantime our own house was being built and we carried out a daily inspection. It was ready early 1950. It had all 'mod cons', including a 'fridge – not so common in those days - which had a capacity of one and a half cubic feet, and was cooled by a gas flame. It was big enough to hold two pints of milk and one or two other things as well. There was of course no central heating but a coke combustion stove in the kitchen to heat the water. The 'garden' was soil and weeds, because in those days the builders built the house but did not set up the garden as well. There was a brick wall round the garden, about two and a bit feet high, so anybody could look in to the garden. We could not afford turf and so we put down some grass seed. We could not afford to furnish more than the lounge and bedroom, and even there our bedside table was a small step-ladder, so it was dual-purpose. Nevertheless it was a tremendous improvement on what had gone before. We had a kitchen table in the dining room – no carpet of course, or light fitting; just the bare bulb – and, at that time, washing machines, both for clothes and dishes, were very rare. We could not have afforded one anyway. To dry clothes we had a pulley on the kitchen ceiling, which could be lowered by a rope to hang things on it, then raised to ceiling height to dry them – and to ensure that they smelt of cooking.

In the meantime Sonia decided to put her own plate up and start her own practice. There as no advertising in those days, and so there was just a discreet plate outside a house in Crosby Village, where Sonia had rented rooms, with the name 'Dr S.H.J. Goldrein' on the plate outside. Had Sonia declared her sex it would, at that time, have put prospective patients off. Indeed one such patient called on her, found that she was a woman, and walked out. We had no car, and for the few patients Sonia had to see – starting at one (me) – a bike was good enough. A friend of ours, Bill Morgan, a barrister, had a large Chrysler which he lent us. We could not afford the petrol actually to use the car, but it looked good standing outside the surgery, as not every house had a car in those days.

In 1951 we had the great unhappiness of our first child being premature and dying after a day or two. It was a terrible shock after all the excitement of expectation, but Sonia, as always, withstood it with tremendous fortitude. Fortunately in August 1952 Iain was born, and we were a family.

In the meantime I went into junior partnership with the firm where I had been working , which then had three partners including me, and I had a one-fifth share of the profits. It ran well, and I was quite content, until the first year's accounts came out. Whilst we had been very busy, and the two senior partners had had house enlargements and expensive foreign holidays, the figures were down. Sonia advised me to investigate, but I told her that everything was in the books and there was no way there could have been any deception. She insisted – rightly – that I should check and an inspection showed that indeed not all the 'take' from certain clients had gone through the books. In addition, and this capped it, I was with one of the partners one day when he charged a client £5 for advice. The client paid him there and then in cash. When the client left he gave me my share - £1. I wondered if I would have received that had I not been in the room at the time, and how many similar payments there had been where my share had not been passed on to me. This client could not, surely, have been the only one paying in cash.

We are not gamblers but we then, in 1953, took a gamble, and decided that I should start on my own in Liverpool. I found a second floor office, with no lift, in the City centre. Sonia came to help clean it and scrub the floors – Iain was in his carry-cot – and we did what we could, furnishing it with second-hand furniture. The plate outside the building, about eighteen inches by about a foot, was dark bronze with white letters, reading 'Goldrein and Co. Solicitors and Commissioners for Oaths'. My friends asked who the 'Co.' was. The Liverpool Law Society came to inspect to ensure that my plate was not so big as to constitute advertising – how different from the present day with illuminated shop-fronts, advertisements on the backs of buses, and notices saying 'Have you had an accident?'. I feel sure that the next move will be for there to be notices which read 'Why don't you have an accident?'. There was absolutely no advertising, and even if Sonia had a patient in the surgery asking if she knew a solicitor, she did not mention my 'firm'. One had to be as careful as that.

I sat and waited hoping a client might come in. My mother came in to pretend to be a secretary and to receive any clients, if they should come. I clearly recall reading 'The Cruel Sea' which took me a day or two, and then suddenly my mother announced that there was a client! She showed him in to my room, in her excitement mistakenly taking him via an undecorated room which looked terrible, but at least he had come. Whilst he was with me my mother was busy knocking at my door to say that there had been a call from the Chief Constable, and asking me to ring back, or that the High Court had been enquiring about a case. If only they had been genuine! I think the client was duly impressed. I could hear the typewriter clattering outside – and I knew that my mother could not type. She was just bashing away at anything to give the right sound.

When the client left she asked me what it was. I said that it was a divorce. She asked me how much it was worth, and I replied 'about £40'. She burst into tears of joy and hugged me.

We had by then managed to get a car, a Ford Prefect, about the cheapest car one could buy. We only managed this because Sonia, as a doctor, had priority, cars at that time being in very short supply. It had only two transverse springs, no boot but a rear luggage rack, no heater, and to let air in you opened a flap in front. In damp weather the windscreen misted up and so we managed to buy a plastic strip, about a foot long, which was held on to the windscreen by rubber suckers and which housed a metal heating strip, which cleared about a square foot of windscreen. There were no door or wing mirrors. And when we drove to Newcastle-upon-Tyne to see Sonia's parents, after driving behind a lorry or even another car, the wet and mud splattered up. The wipers merely smeared it, and so we carried rags and bottles of water to enable us to clean the windscreen every few miles until it happened again. The screen-washer had not been invented. The rear window misted up very quickly. We managed to afford an oval piece of plastic which had rubber round the edges and a sucker in the middle. This was pressed on to the glass leaving a sealed space inside the plastic oval which did not, if you were lucky, mist up.

Sonia's practice gradually grew and at the end of my first year I had actually made a small living. By then I had two telephone lines, a secretary of course, and an office boy. It was a big wage bill for me but I was making enough to cover it. I remember complaining to Sonia after about a year in practice that I had received an income tax return form.

Sonia told me that I should not complain, but I should be delighted, because it confirmed that I had an income!

I clearly recall my first appearance in the County Court as an advocate. Sonia came with me to judge how I did – at my request of course. I had prepared my opening address to the Judge. I could not prepare the closing address as I did not know what evidence would be given. This being so, my closing speech had to be off-the-cuff. After the case, which I won, Sonia told me that my opening address was very adequate, but my closing address was excellent. Since then I have always worked from notes and have never read a prepared speech.

Both our practices were on the 'up' and in 1954 Sonia presented me with Nadine, as lovely a daughter as Iain was a son. Sonia had been visiting patients the evening before she was born – she had done the same with Iain – and in each case got to hospital just in time.

People used to stop the pram in the street for both of them. This meant, of course, that Sonia had a home, a practice, and two babies to look after. As always she took it all in her stride, and that fact that the practice was still comparatively small was good, because otherwise her life would have been impossible. Iain was a bottom-shuffler – that meant that he never crawled but used to shuffle along the floor on his bottom with great skill and speed. We felt that we could have made use of that by allowing him to sit on a duster and put him in the kitchen. He could have cleaned the floor in a flash!

I could give you an interesting history of the children, their children and their grand-children, but that would be a book on its own, and so I hope that they will forgive me if I do not follow up their careers.

It was suggested at that time that I should join the local golf club – although I had never played golf - as I would be able to make contacts who might discover that I was a solicitor. I was not keen but I was pressed to apply and so I did. After about three months I asked my proposer, who had been so insistent, what was the score. He told me, rather abashed, that he had been asked to withdraw my nomination as otherwise I would be black-balled. I asked the reason, as I could think of no black marks against me. He reluctantly admitted that the reason was that I was Jewish, and that they would not accept Jewish members. In recent years they would take any members – even Jews – but I could not join a club which had behaved in that way.

In the mid-fifties I was constantly complaining about poor local services and criticising the local authority for what they failed to do. My father-in-law said that if I was so dissatisfied I should go on the Council myself and put things right from the inside. As a youngster I had been a socialist and, indeed, I had been the Pembroke College Secretary of the Cambridge University Socialist Club – and I voted Labour when I was old enough to vote. However I had become so disillusioned that I had changed colours, and so I approached the Conservative Party. I was readily adopted – I had not realised that as a Cambridge graduate, an ex-officer and a solicitor I was a good candidate to project.

We started the door-to-door canvassing, and in those days there were public meetings with speeches, a part which I thoroughly enjoyed. I used to have notes but never a prepared speech as, if there were barrackers, it was easier to deal with them and then carry on speaking rather than being tied to a script. I remember one candidate who read his speech from a script. He was frequently interrupted, as we all were, but he always had a job to find his place to carry on where he had left off. This confirmed to me, if I needed confirmation, that prepared scripts were out.

To get back to the election, I got in with a majority of about 60 in what was a marginal ward, and there I was, Councillor Goldrein, on the Crosby Borough Council. Fairly soon I was asked to be Housing Chairman having made, I suppose, some sort of a mark – I do not know what sort – on the other councillors. This was a time when high rise flats were coming it, and we had a housing backlog which could have been solved, it seemed to me, with 'system building' – prefabricated parts which could quickly and more cheaply be erected into tall blocks. I had seen some of these in Liverpool and nearby and had not liked them either for their facilities or for their appearance. So I went with the Housing Manager – Mr Salthouse, there being no first names in those days – to various parts of the country and Scotland, with time I could hardly afford, because the practice was getting busier, and eventually saw what I thought was right. Of course in those days councillors did not get paid; it was purely voluntary.

We had a Council meeting to decide whether or not to proceed. The cost was, even then, some millions, but it went through in a few minutes. The next item on the agenda was whether we should pay £7 or £11 for street seats, but this took well over half an hour. The problem was that the councillors could understand a few pounds, but millions were much more difficult. The blocks were duly built, they are to this day acceptable, whilst many of those in Liverpool and elsewhere have been demolished.

There was not just this system-building, as it was called. There were other housing problems, and other types of deprivation. There was one deprived area in my Ward known as Little Scandinavia, as it consisted of Norway, Sweden and Denmark Streets. We regularly canvassed there and were lucky to get away with our lives.

These people were rehoused and I can fairly say that by the end of my time as Chairman of Housing the housing problem in the Borough had been solved. There was still a lot to do to keep it running though – what to do, for example, with problem families. Were they all to be grouped together in the same block, and labelled, or were they to be spread about possibly bringing problems to non-problem families? We in fact effected compromises which worked well.

By this time in the office I had taken in various articled clerks – trainee solicitors today – who were a big help at, in those days, no cost – and then I took an assistant solicitor, Jack Levin, who later became my first partner. That took away a chunk of my profits but, of course, in the longer term it was essential and paid off. We were together for many years.

Indeed the practice was growing and we had taken additional rooms on the same second floor, and also on the first floor. We really had a staff and were coming be recognized as a go-ahead firm in Liverpool. The practice grew to the extent that in 1963 we moved to far more prestigious offices in Victoria Street, a bank building, with a lift and we took a whole floor. By this time, as well, I had been elected to the Lancashire County Council, and so with my professional and civic work and the family, which always came first, there was a lot to do. I remember one morning coming downstairs for breakfast when Sonia, standing in the hall, said 'Wait a minute, haven't I seen your face somewhere before?'!

In the meantime both our practices were growing. Nevertheless when I was invited to be the Mayor Crosby in 1966 I was very happy to accept, particularly as I was the youngest person to fill that office in the history of the Borough. Mayors, like other councillors, were not, of course, paid in those days, and everything was voluntary. I preferred that, and I still do, because it gave one a chance to give something to society without taking. I am not, I hope, being self-righteous, but it meant as well that I could look anybody in the face with no embarrassment knowing that there was nothing in it for me. As the Mayor I was given the sum of £5000 to cover entertaining and clothing for both of us – at that time the Mayor always wore either full evening dress or morning coat, with black or grey topper as was appropriate, and Sonia had to have a very varied wardrobe because people commented on what the Mayoress was wearing. The £5000 helped, but it cost us a fair sum too. But it was worth it.

--oOo--

Chapter 11
His Worship The Mayor

O f course in the United Kingdom at that time, as today, the Mayor had no power. He was more like a constitutional monarch, opening factories, attending charities, kissing babies, chairing the Council Meetings, attending garden parties, church services, school speech days, visits to factories and offices, laying foundation stones – the lot. The first major function, not unreasonably, was the Mayor-making ceremony. It was held in the Alexandra Hall, the largest civic hall, where the then Mayor introduced me. I put on his robe and he put on the robe of the Deputy Mayor, and then I had to make my inaugural speech.

The press had, a few days before, asked me for a copy of my speech. I was a little surprised as I thought that they would be able to take it down in shorthand – there were no tape recorders or other electronic aids in those days to help them. They said that they really would prefer a copy of it.

I had a case at that time in the Chester Assizes, where a client of mine was charged with corrupting a member of one of the Borough Councils in the Wirral – which case incidentally in due course I won. I was driving to and from Chester each day for several days, and so rather than sit in the car – car radios were not particularly good in those days – I decided to think out my speech. After a few days the ideas had crystallised and I made a few headings, as I usually did for a speech. Then I went through it in my mind and it worked out to the twenty minutes or so that were required.

I had it typed up and gave it to the press. After the mayor-making ceremony I asked them if it had been anywhere near the mark or wildly different. I was relieved – and surprised – to learn that it was nearly verbatim. This was followed by the mayoral lunch and more speeches. I had arranged that the catering should be Kosher so that my Jewish guests, and I, would be able to eat with no problems. I have not such a great belief that I might suffer eternal damnation if I ate non-kosher food, nor indeed if I broke some of the other rules, but at the same time I was not, and still am not, prepared to break a chain of tradition after some 3,500 years. And so kosher food was served. My chaplain was Rabbi Wolfe, from my Synagogue, Princes Road. I told him that I would like him to say the Jewish grace before the meal. He said 'In English, of course'. I replied that it would be in Hebrew, as it should be, and he did so. The public thoroughly enjoyed the novelty. The fact is that I am Jewish and so I saw, and see, no reason to hide it. I have always found indeed that I have gained far more respect than I would have done by pretence.

Being the Mayor meant in practice that I had to attend several functions a day, and that was apart from the office and other professional commitments. I had one problem with church services, high or low. That was that the Mayor always had the seat of honour, and nobody would stand up or sit down before he did – and this 'he' had insufficient knowledge of church services to know when these moments arose. I learned quickly – because I had to. When it came to standing one could get a 'feel' of the people round about, the hand on the book-rest in front straining to get up, the anxious looks. The same applied to sitting down. I soon got the hang of it and to this day would be able to sit/stand at most services of most churches at the right time.

I arranged a special Civil Service at my Synagogue in Princes Road, with all the aldermen and councillors, and the formality of the mace and attendants. I had tremendous support from them all, and as the only Jew my beliefs were given the greatest respect. I have always had the view that if you respect yourself and your beliefs, and are not 'hush-hush' about it, you have more chance of receiving the respect of others, and I did.

There was a very pleasant limousine provided for us – in fact there were two, in case the Mayoress was going to one place and the Mayor to another. We had a chauffeur and a mace-bearer, who were always with us and a 'spare' chauffer if we needed one. Often, when going to or from a function, we could go via a house where Sonia had to see a patient, she would take off her chain and replace it with stethoscopes, do the visit, and come out again to the car and back went the chain. Sometimes she, or we, would stop at the schools to pick up the children from school, take them wherever they had to go, and then continue with our duties. And then there was their homework and the other obligations to the kids.

The chains were never left with us as they were too valuable, and at the end of each session or function they were taken from us and locked in the Town Hall safe. The Mayoress's chain was quite unique, being the only one in the country which bore the Royal Arms. This was, I was told, because the King at the time the Borough was incorporated, Edward VII, was recovering from appendicitis – quite a serious operation in those days –and when asked if the Borough could use the Royal Arms he was probably prepared to agree to anything within reason, and so he agreed to this request.

The idea of being elected Mayor had been attractive and immediately accepted, but I did not realise until later what I had let myself – and Sonia – in for. I had my work in the office as senior partner, and despite the mayoral year I remained the biggest earner, so clearly I had to get down to work despite the time pressure. I was a member of the Lancashire County Council, which involved committee and Council meetings in Preston, the best part of an hour's drive away. That meant two hours' travel plus Council time whenever there was something on. In addition I was the 'Second in Command', otherwise known as the Junior Warden, of our Synagogue, and now I had added on to all these the functions of the Mayor.

The most formal of all, of course, were the Council meetings, to confirm or debate all the decisions of the committees. I am a punctual person, on the basis that punctuality is the courtesy of kings and the politeness of princes. I started on time. Councillors were accustomed to roll in up to ten or fifteen minutes late. At my first Council meeting we finished in twenty minutes, there being so few councillors there that there were few, if any, speeches regarding the various resolutions.

Those who rolled up late just had to do without! They learned their lesson and thereafter they arrived on time and the Council meetings, naturally, went on for longer because there were more members there to raise all sorts of points – which were frequently pointless!

Sonia had her share of problems too. She had the house to run, the children, and her surgeries and house visits. At the same time she had to be with me on very many occasions, and very often, too, she was invited to functions where the Mayoress was required on her own. That meant that she had to make speeches too. Neither of us used - although we were offered – speech writers, and we had to dress appropriately for each occasion.

Matters were made easier by the mayoral attendants. Mr Brindle (I never knew his first name) was the Mace Bearer, and Jack Shankland, an absolute gem and a perfect gentleman, was the mayoral chauffeur. He had started life as a miner but I have rarely, if ever, met a more gentlemanly gentleman. He looked after us with loving care, was always on time and always at the right place, and yet always appeared to be unflustered and unhurried. In addition there was the Mayor's Secretary, Miss Firth (I never knew her first name either) and she, again, was a gem. We have, over all the years, kept in touch with Jack Shankland who fought the War from Dunkirk to Normandy and to Berlin without a scratch. As I write this he is ninety, and I hope he has many more years to come.

The typical day ran from rising at about seven in the morning, and we were lucky to be in bed by midnight. One of the problems was not to over-eat or over-drink. The average mayor put on about a stone in weight during the year of office. We made a point of being abstemious, which is not always easy, and this applied to the drinks as well. I would continue to hold the full glass most of the evening, or hide it away behind a curtain or somewhere equally convenient, and when offered another glass I could graciously accept it – and not drink that either. I remember one of my receptions where the neighbouring mayors were guests – we used to be called 'the chain gang'. One – I will not mention from where – was on one occasion so drunk that he could not even remember having gone down to the main hall for the food.

Some events were, of course, more outstanding than others. One was the Remembrance Parade in Crosby, marching solemnly to the War Memorial and placing the wreath to remember those from Crosby who died in the two wars. It was very moving. Another was the Jewish Ex-Servicemen's Parade in London, the week after Remembrance Sunday. Jack Shankland drove us down and we had a couple of stops on the motorway for refreshments. We always had Jack join us, and to our amazement we found that this had not been the custom on out-of-town visits by other mayors. He was such a gentleman that we preferred his company to many of the higher-ranking people whom we came across.

He got to London and although he had hardly been to the Big City before, he went straight to Horse Guards' Parade, which was the first stop. The next stop was the Home Office and he had the presence of mind to hook on to, and follow, the Lord Mayor of Westminster's car. He felt sure that that chauffeur knew the way, and felt that if he followed him he could not go wrong. He did just that, and was always in the right place at the right time. Then during the march past Sonia and I were standing on the steps of the Home Office as those on the parade went by and saluted.

All this, with factory visits and everything else, made the year fly by. There was not a moment to spare and we delighted in it all. There were sad times, like the MenCap Christmas party, where the parents were really wonderful with their retarded children, there were the old people who were delighted to be noticed, the school-children who were surprised that we took a real interest – in fact whilst there were many grand occasions, it was the visits to these people which were really moving and satisfying. They were being noticed, an interest was being taken in them, and these occasions were really meaningful.

I had the privilege of planting a tree on the occasion of the opening of a new wing of the Roman Catholic Park House Nursing Home, with Bishop Harris, the Suffragan Roman Catholic Bishop of Liverpool. We got to know each other quite well, and some time later I expressed my pity for him in that the front of his cassock had some dozens of buttons, and I sympathised with him on the work involved when he had to robe – because after all it was not right that a man of the cloth should have had a personal valet. He smiled and said: 'We may not be as old as Jerusalem, but we have discovered the zip fastener!'.

We attending the consecration of two cathedrals – and not many cities have two. There was the great new Anglican Cathedral in Liverpool near the City centre, said to be the largest Anglican Cathedral in Europe, and the new Roman Catholic Cathedral. This was, and of course is, most unusual, round, with the altar in the middle and surmounted by vertical stained glass windows at the top of the tapering roof. The round building with the crown on the roof gave it the title, with typical Liverpool humour, of 'Heenan's wigwam', named after the then Roman Catholic Archbishop. Its other title was 'The Mersey Funnel'.

The Mayoral year was not the end of it. The following year I was Deputy Mayor, which was quite a good idea because instead of coming to a sudden stop you had a gradual easing-off. The Deputy Mayor, and Deputy Mayoress, attended functions when the Mayor had a double booking, was away, ill and so on. The year clearly was not as busy as the full Mayoral duties, but nevertheless was quite a time-consumer, still full of interest, and yet at the end of the winding-down it was easier to slip back to a normal day.

Life then returned to the fairly normal, with Crosby Borough Council and Lancashire County Council to keep me out of mischief. Having been Mayor I had, of course, ceased to be Chairman of the Housing Committee. The next vacancy to arise was the Baths Committee, not terribly interesting but it brought me back to the realities of the Council. Unfortunately the swimming baths, which were new, had been designed by the Borough Architect. He was a lovely chap and a good architect, but a swimming bath requires certain special skills which he did not possess. First the main pool was 100 yards long, when international, and indeed national, swimming, was by then being measured in metres. The beautiful under-water viewing ports were never in fact used as no real competitions could take place in a non-metric pool. Another problem was the floor tiles, which became slippery and caused accidents. Indeed on one occasion Sonia slipped and fell at the pool side. The windows had metal frames which rusted. Eventually in the early 2000s it was demolished to make way for something properly designed.

Then an opportunity arose which I found much more attractive – the Town Planning Committee. There, I felt, I could make a difference and it was a welcome challenge. There had been, and indeed still are, many large old houses in the Borough with large grounds and garden areas. These were being sold to developers as many people could no longer afford such large residences, and the developers, not unreasonably, wishing to make as much money as possible, had been building flats. There could be as many as thirty or forty flats on the site of one home. The density in the 'desirable residential areas' was increasing alarmingly.

Soon after I took the Chair a further similar application came along, and the Borough officers strongly recommended that we should grant it. I expressed my severe misgivings as to density, but they said firmly that if we refused planning permission, the developers would appeal and win. I suggested that we refuse and put it to the test. We did that. The developers appealed. We won. Houses were built on that site instead of flats – I think on that particular site it was about five houses.

This set the pattern and during my tenure no planning consents were given for the erection of blocks of flats in low-density residential areas. Unfortunately my successor as Chairman acceded to the suggestions of the officers and once again the high density development restarted. It is interesting to note that as long afterwards as 2002 a similar problem arose, the local population objected strongly, and were successful.

Then in 1970 at the Local Government elections, the Conservatives were doing badly country-wide. When there was a Conservative Government, and the same applies today, local government always went to the left, and vice versa if there were a Labour government, and my seat, which had always been marginal, giving me a majority sometimes of double figures only, was lost to Labour and, in fact, never regained. So I was left with the Lancashire County Council.

I continued to attend the various meetings but it continued to be dull. The powers that were, that is the Chairman and the Chief Executive, decided that as the details of the committee decisions were so bulky they could not send them to every member, and so we could collect them at County Hall and peruse them before the Council meeting on the day. The papers were over a foot high and so clearly this was impossible and so nobody read them with the result that these world-shattering decisions were made on an uninformed vote without discussion or argument. The whole Council meeting took about a half-hour, apart from saying farewell to dead councillors and hello to new ones. But there was something much more exciting on the horizon, and that was the Government's proposal to introduce Metropolitan Counties. Ours was to be The County of Merseyside, and would include Liverpool, Crosby, Southport, Formby, Bootle, St Helens, the Wirral peninsular, and Knowsley, with a total population of some one and a quarter million people. Crosby, Bootle, Formby and Southport were to become the Borough of Sefton, and I was asked – and readily agreed – to stand as a candidate for the northern part of Crosby, a far safer seat than I had ever had before. And, surprise surprise, I won it!

The elections took place in 1973 for the County Council to commence working in 1974. Having been elected we could start the preparations and we chose as Party Leader – there was really little choice - Sir Kenneth Thompson, Bart, who had been a government minister and hence was the obvious choice. To my great surprise I was elected Deputy Leader, and we duly started putting our teams together. We knew from the election results that we would be the Opposition, but the County of Merseyside was a big and interesting responsibility which made it worthwhile.

As Deputy Leader, and as the Conservative Party spokesman on Highways, I was kept pretty busy, and at that time my firm had grown to six offices. There we had regular partners' meetings but, naturally, as senior partner I had a lot to do in that direction and a lot of administration to control. I still managed, though, to be the biggest earner in the practice.

Then, late in 1972, I received a letter from the Lord Chancellor's Department to say that I had been appointed a Deputy Circuit Judge. Knowing that solicitors were not eligible to sit as judges in the Crown and County Courts I concluded that there had been a mistake, and I telephoned the Lord Chancellor's office to say so. I spoke to a senior civil servant who told me that the law had recently been changed enabling solicitors to be appointed, and that I was one of the first to be chosen. I was very flattered, but a little concerned as I had not even set foot in a Crown Court for some twenty years. I had been busy with civil work, and crime was delegated to others.

The first hurdle was that I was asked to attend a sentencing conference in London – a one-day conference for all new appointees to the judiciary, full-time or part-time. I checked the date and found that it was on the second day of the Jewish festival of the New Year, Rosh HaShana, one of the holiest days in the Jewish calendar. I telephoned the Lord Chancellor's Office to say that there were doubtless other Jewish judges who would be in the same position and would be unable to attend the conference on that day. He said that he understood completely and would telephone all the other Jewish judges to ask their views, and that if they felt the same the date of the Conference would be moved. One could not ask for more than that. A few days later he telephoned me regretting that none of the others had complained, and they were prepared to attend. What annoyed me particularly was that some months later I met one of those Jewish appointees who attended, busy mouthing his prayers and giving the outward impression of religious devotion, when I knew full well the measure of his hypocrisy.

This delayed the start of my sitting by six months, until the next conference was held, but in the meantime I sat with the Recorder of Manchester, next to him on the bench, to get the feel of the proceedings, to work out the procedures and get an idea of the sentences he was imposing.

At last the sentencing conference arrived, and then I was able to take my place on the Bench. I had already bought my wig and on the first day, duly bewigged and robed I was in my Chambers when the usher came in and asked if I was ready. I told him I was. Then to my surprise he went up to a door – not the one through which I had come but the one which I then I realised led to the courtroom – and he gave it three loud knocks from the inside. Then he opened the door and called out in a loud voice, 'All stand', and indicated to me to go in.

I remembered where the judge sat – in the middle in front - and anyway it was the only vacant seat up there. I went to the seat and was about to sit down when I felt that nobody else was moving to be seated, neither the clerk nor counsel nor the solicitors and others in the court.

Maybe it was my experience as Mayor, when attending church services, which came to my aid. I hesitated, and it was a good job I did. Suddenly the usher called in a loud voice, 'All those who have matters before Her Majesty's judges draw near and give your attention. God save the Queen and Her Majesty's judges'. I then felt that it was now the right time to sit down. I did, and everybody else did the same, so obviously I had done the right thing, but it had been a near thing to being a major clanger, particularly as I had no doubt that the barristers appearing before me would in any case be very doubtful as to the ability of a solicitor to carry out judicial duties, never having been involved in them before.

The day started and the first case was called on, and I remembered enough to be able to handle it. However after a couple of hours I felt that I needed to go to the 'Boys' room'. The judge cannot really say 'I want to spend a penny', and so I decided to speak to the jury in a most paternal and judicial manner, being concerned for their well-being. I said 'Members of the jury, some of you would no doubt wish to have a short natural break'. They whispered among themselves and then one of them replied, on behalf of them all, 'No, thank you very much your Honour, we are all perfectly comfortable'. So I suffered until the luncheon adjournment. I never made that mistake again – thereafter I said 'Members, of the jury, I have no doubt that some of you would like a natural break, and so I am adjourning for five minutes'. That worked a treat.

I started my first trial. The jury was sworn in, I heard opening speeches, and found to my delight that I was able to control counsel and witnesses politely but firmly, and found that in return I was well-received by those appearing before me. I was very relieved because barristers have been known to have a modicum of arrogance, and I was the first solicitor before whom they had ever appeared, and yet it ran well and the relationship was good. Indeed I can say that in all the years I sat I was always well received despite being firm and running the court my way. I was very pleased, as well, at the luncheon adjournment on the second day when an old barrister friend of mine from Liverpool, who was also sitting as a judge, told me that I had gone down well! There had been no clangers and even a solicitor could get it right!

I sat in the Crown and County Courts trying crime, civil and divorce cases, for a number of years. I was known for rather heavy sentencing but that was because I always had in mind the rules for the reduction of sentences for 'good conduct', sometimes up to a half or a third. There were about ten appeals against the sentences I imposed but not one of them was successful. One appeal related to a case when I was sitting in the Derby Crown Court – I used to go to such far-away places. I forget the details but I clearly recall that the offence was serious and certainly warranted a substantial sentence. I sentenced him to ten years. The family at the back of the court started to shout threats and the police immediately took them out of court. I do not know what happened to them after that. After we rose the Police Inspector came to my chambers to ask me if I wanted an escort out of town – it was Friday afternoon. I declined, saying that on removing my wig and gown, which I described as my 'fancy dress', nobody would recognize me anyway – and nobody did.

Sometimes inevitably the County Council crossed the path of the Crown and County Courts, but fortunately not too often. One afternoon I was dealing with matrimonial cases – these days called 'Family Law' – in chambers. In the middle of the case my telephone rang, and I realised that it must be important for them to interrupt me in the middle of a hearing. It was the County Treasurer, Peter Jenkins. We, at the County Council, had been considering acquisitions of properties for the County's Pension Fund, and a most urgent decision was required as to whether or not we should buy a large office block, Castle Chambers, in Liverpool City Centre, a most desirable acquisition, and the decision had to be made that afternoon. The price was £2 million, which in those days was a lot, and I mean a lot, of money. I did a quick calculation, made a quick decision, gave the O.K., and within about three minutes I continued the case where I had left off. It is curious how the mind can switch from one thing to the other, with no trespassing on either side.

But during this time there were certain privileges to be derived from the various political jobs, and among the best of these were the Royal Garden parties. We had been invited to our first one when I was Mayor of Crosby, and in later years went to four more due, says he pompously, to my elevated position in the various Councils on which I served. There were three a year and about 7000 guests at each, which meant that some 21,000 people, if my mathematics are correct, attended each year. It is a comparatively cheap way of rewarding people, gives them great pleasure, and I think that there is no country in the world which can offer such an 'honour', about which you tell all your friends – and enemies – at so little cost.

You have to, or at least are advised to, dress in morning coat, which makes you feel good anyway, and to walk in through the gates of the Palace with the public looking on and wondering who you are – I would never risk telling them because that would destroy the magic – and into the Palace: Then straight through the beautiful hallways to the Terrace and the gardens, where there were numerous pink flamingos round the lake. They have gone now, I think, because some disease struck them.

There is a large marquee where you can have canapés, tea, coffee, cakes and there are tables where you can sit and relax. Just behind there is another marquee which contains the loos, but very nice ones, with attendants dressed in tails with brass buttons and very much 'royal servants' brushing you down as you leave. Behind the marquees was a large van with the sign on the side, 'J. Lyons - Royal Catering'. In that respect the Royal Family is very democratic and it was the same J. Lyons catering which you could get anywhere.

Officers of the Honourable Corps of Gentlemen at Arms, dressed in morning coat but wearing carnations in their button-holes, and a few Yeomen of the Guard – the Beefeaters - started moving and indicating where we should stand. There were no words, just indications, but very clear ones. So you get in what you think will be the right position and then the Queen, the Duke of Edinburgh, and other members of the Royal Family come on to the Terrace. The Guards' Band plays the National Anthem.

Various people were presented to them on the terrace and then the Queen led the Royal Party down to the gardens, where we were by now arranged in 'lanes', with the Gentlemen-at-Arms gently keeping us in the right places. You may be in the Queen's lane – the most crowded and so you see less if you are at the back, or the Prince of Wales and so on. The 'Gentlemen' then bring members of the audience out to the middle of the lane to be presented to the particular Royal, where they have a chat and then return to the side. It looks as if they do that at random but in fact it is all arranged beforehand and the presentees know that they are going to be presented.

Some of the minor Royals have fewer people round them and so are more approachable. We were in this way presented to the Prince of Wales and Prince and Princess Michael of Kent, on different occasions. The meeting with the Kents was just after the Toxteth Riots in Liverpool in 1981. There had been a lot of damage there and serious injuries. One man was killed. Princess Michael was charming and asked Sonia's medical advice regarding her cold, but the Prince, being told that we came from Liverpool, asked me how things were after the riots. I explained that they had been very serious and traumatic for the City. He said that it was unfortunate that the parents did not keep the children and young people at home watching television rather than that they should be out in the streets.

I respectfully pointed out that in Toxteth the standards to which he, and indeed we, were accustomed, hardly applied and that we were talking of a different world. He seemed unable to grasp this, and said 'Well, perhaps it is like the skate-board craze, and no doubt they will soon get over it'. I was aghast and astonished at his lack of touch with the 'common people', and if I had not heard it myself I would not have believed it.

The Royal Party, as a series of individuals, made their way gradually towards the Royal Tent, where they all converged and went inside for tea. It was – and it was the same on the other occasions when we were there - rather like a marquee at a Cambridge College Garden Party but rather better and with fewer people - but why not? The guests who were not invited into the marquee – the vast majority - either stood and stared, had a cup of tea themselves in their marquee, or wandered round the gardens and herbaceous borders. All the Royals in due course returned to the Terrace by a shorter route, waved 'good afternoon', and went back inside the Palace.

On one occasion we took Nadine with us. You can take one unmarried daughter under 21 – not a son – presumably from the days when the Royal Family were looking for spouses for their sons and families. I broke the rules by taking a small camera in too, and took some pictures with it holding it concealed under my grey topper. They came out very well, but I wonder what the consequences would have been had I been caught. At another Garden Party later on I tried the same thing, but in case the camera bulged in my pocket I gave it to Sonia to put in her handbag. They had not searched handbags before. They did this time. They very courteously took it from me to return it on departure. That was the last of the five Parties we went to, but had there been a sixth I think I would have tried my trouser pocket.

But in the meantime the Merseyside County Council had its serious sides and serious problems as well. We were the Local Authority overriding all others, the most important responsibilities being Highways, Police, Fire Service, Arts and Culture and the overall Planning Authority. We were also involved in the economic growth of Merseyside. I clearly recall one morning walking with Audrey Lees, the Chief Planning Officer, round the old Albert Dock. These docks had been built in Victorian times, and were in brick, massive, with inland docks as well where the sailing ships, and the steamships of the time, could sail. The walls were thick, the floors were thick, there were hydraulic pipes all over as they provided the power before electricity came in, and as I said to Audrey, if we left them just as they were, after rendering them safe, they were a museum as they stood. You could almost feel the ships coming, the masses of people and cargoes, a tremendous buzz of activity.

We tried various means to get entrepreneurs to put in money to develop the docks, but, as usual, there were lots of promises but no action. Indeed when Ken Thompson was the Leader we had a 'celebratory' tour of the river in the ferry boat, 'The Royal Iris', to encourage one such entrepreneur to come to some agreement. That was as far as it got.

In 1977 there were the County Council elections. We worked hard and canvassed hard. We had the advantage of there being a Labour government which always helps the opposition parties at local government elections. I remember so clearly being at the County Headquarters as the results came in, and there were more and more blue patches until it became clear that we had won. It was hard to realise that we had won at all in Merseyside, but we never expected it to be to the extent that we had sixty-seven out of the ninety-nine seats on the Council. So Ken Thompson was the Leader of the Council and I was his Deputy.

It worked out satisfactorily but after a time there were rumblings that Ken Thompson's autocracy was not conducive to good relations within our Party. Ken did not want to relinquish his job but the majority desired that he should. A compromise was reached: Previously the Leader of the Party in power was also Chairman of the County Council. So it was decided, and he rather reluctantly agreed, to become the Chairman, with no powers other than formal ones and to be the 'referee' at Council meetings, and I was, after a contested election within the Party, appointed Leader of the Council.

After I became Leader we were fortunate that Michael Heseltine – later Lord Heseltine - was appointed Secretary of State for the Environment, with a particular responsibility for Merseyside. I knew him well and he had spoken on my election platforms, and so no introductions were necessary. He used to come up about once a week and he stayed at the Atlantic Tower Hotel, and I joined him usually either for breakfast or dinner to discuss what we could do. He did very many things for Merseyside and I cannot remember his ever saying 'no'. The first time we met for dinner there were four of us – he was with Timothy Sainsbury, his Parliamentary Private Secretary, and I was with another senior member of the Council. When we got to the table I noticed that Michael had so arranged the round table that he was at the head! He had allowed more space on each side of him, so that he stood out. I pulled his leg mercilessly and he never did that again – he was in fact such a man that wherever he sat was the head of the table.

After some discussions he established the Merseyside Development Corporation, the first one in the country, its task being to regenerate the County. I immediately brought up the question of the Albert Dock, and it became the most important part of his agenda. A Board was set up, Government money was made available, and these magnificent dock buildings became a living museum. Apart from shops and boutiques there are offices, television studios, blocks of flats – all in the old dock buildings – and including the Tate Gallery of the North, and the magnificent Liverpool Maritime Museum. There is, too, a Museum of Liverpool Life, little ferry boats, guided tours, hotels and very adequate car parking. If I look back on my political life I can look back on the Albert Dock development with great satisfaction and with the knowledge that I had something to do with it.

But the Merseyside Development Corporation went far beyond this, and together we sorted out the Merseyside Garden Festival. This was the utilization of more and more of the old dock area as the Garden Festival site. The land had been used as a tip for many years, and this led to methane gas seeping through and being potentially dangerous. This had to be collected and channelled, and the overall idea, which really happened, was that there should be a promenade south right up to the area of Otterspool, pubs, offices, houses, an exhibition hall, and delightful landscaping. It was incredible that the whole area which had been completely derelict suddenly became a prime part of the City of Liverpool, apart from giving a quick road route to the southern part of the City.

In the meantime we had another major distraction in that our son Iain decided to marry Margaret de Haas, a young barrister living in London but born in Rhodesia, which later became, of course, Zimbabwe. Iain had been to Cambridge and Margaret to Bristol University, but they met in London. It was a good match because to live with a lawyer can be difficult, and to live with a barrister is even more difficult because of the odd hours and the fact that one can suddenly be called on to do a 'job'. A solicitor can pass work on to a partner or assistant, but a barrister is on his or her own and if a case overruns and ruins the family holiday, there is nothing he or she can do about it. And so it was a good arrangement as they both understood the problems, and fortunately they made a success of it.

At about the same time the new Law Courts were built to replace those used in St George's Hall, where the accommodation was 'bitty' having been added to and rooms adapted over many years, and that could now revert to being a very beautiful edifice with a magnificent hall, with one of the biggest, if not the biggest, organ in Europe, a fantastic floor, and the two old great law courts were kept for display purposes. There had been, under the Hall, the cells where the prisoners were kept until their cases were called, and these are now part of the sight-seeing tour.

The new Court building was large and impressive, and was opened by Her Majesty, and named the 'Queen Elizabeth II Law Courts' – popularly known as the 'QE 2'. But just before that she opened the 1984 Garden Festival, and we were all seated ready for the great occasion. Sonia suddenly pointed out a man in casual and bizarre clothes – to put it at its smartest – with large gold earrings and with a Mexican style haircut in red, green and orange She said to me 'Who on earth is that?', as he waved across to me. I, deadpan, said, 'Oh, he's from Conservative Central Office'! In fact he was the Director of the Everyman Theatre trying, clearly, to be 'with it' in a 'with it' theatre. From there we went across to the Court building where again there was a formal opening with presentations to the Queen and the Duke of Edinburgh. What was quite moving for me was that Liverpool, which had been down in the dumps for some years, was really showing signs of revival, and it was being recognized.

One most memorable event was the Queen's Silver Jubilee. She came to Merseyside and as Leader of the Conservative Party – we were by this time again in opposition - I had the privilege of contact with her. She was on the Royal Iris, one of the Mersey ferry boats, with a party of VIPs – including me! I was presented with others and then I was on the dais on the deck with her. There was a crowd on the quayside calling out 'Give us a wave, give us a wave', but she did not flutter an eyelid. I said tactfully that 'perhaps, Ma'am, you could give them a wave which would be very much appreciated'. She looked at me as if I had made a dreadful suggestion and did nothing. A little later she did, indeed, give a slight wave, and the crowd cheered and cheered.

There was a concert at the Philharmonic Hall in the evening which the Queen and the Duke of Edinburgh attended. At the interval I was chatting, with others, to her, and she was rather stiff, leaving us to make the running. Then Sonia and I managed to edge over to the Duke of Edinburgh who was quite delightful. He admired Sonia's Ex-Mayoress of Crosby's brooch, and I explained that the Blundells of Crosby were descended from an illegitimate line of John of Gaunt, 'not', as I said to the Duke, 'the sort of pedigree you would appreciate'. His reply was that there had been so many illegitimate lines in the royal family, that he was not one to criticise! We then chatted among other things about beer-bellies – which he said the Australians called "'dockers' goitres" - and the whole session was a delight.

There was another occasion when the new main Police Station was opened in the City centre, and again we were presented, and chatted after tea with the Duke and the Queen. We had been formally presented to the Queen outside and were reintroduced after tea by the Chief Constable as 'Councillor Neville Goldrein and his wife Dr Sonia Goldrein'. I added that 'as Your Majesty has her personal physician in attendance at all times, I have my personal physician with me as well'. The fleeting look on her face was whether to ignore me, laugh, or retort. She chose to laugh and peace was made. A pleasant chatty session followed.

One of Liverpool's main problems was that its main industry had been the docks, which stretched for some seventeen miles. The Port had employed some 25,000 workers. With the advent of containers the docks were very considerably reduced in size – that was one reason for the south docks being developed as the Garden Festival site, as these docks were no longer required for their original purpose. The great problem was that the 25,000 dock workers were no longer needed, and the present workforce is no more than 500, but handling over 35,000,000 tons of cargo a year, more than ever before. It takes some doing by a local economy to swallow up and absorb such a workforce, but before the 'swallowing up' there was a strike of the dockers which went on for two years, and achieved precisely nothing.

Another problem at that time was Liverpool City Council. It had gone very very left wing, and the Leader was John Hamilton, a retired schoolmaster. He was a very nice man, and he admitted to me that he did it for the money because by that time councillors were beginning to get paid – the only thing Michael Heseltine ever did with which I disagreed. To digress for a moment, and we are now in the early 1980s, the Leader of the County Council became entitled to £1000 per year – quite a lot at the time – and the Leader of the Opposition, which was me by then, was entitled to £500. I was not being self-righteous but I had always done my 'public service' because I wanted to do it and I felt that remuneration would kill the spirit of the volunteer. So I decided at the next County Council meeting to say that I did not wish to accept it. I duly did that. The reply from the Labour Leader of the Council was 'Don't worry, we had decided not to offer it to you!'.

In the Highways scene we constructed among other things the Bidston Bye-pass, an important junction in the Wirral. When the grand opening day came I was asked by the contractors, Nuttals, to cut the ribbon, and to close the ceremony they presented me with a delightful pair of cufflinks, in gold with an 'N' in green enamel. The 'N', of course, was for Nuttalls, the contractors. It also stood, of course, for Neville. The problem was that there was a rule, which I strenuously enforced, that any presents to any of the Councillors or officers were the property of the County and were to be displayed in showcases. But who would see a small pair of cufflinks? Who would take any notice? Well, I would, because they bore my initial! They were irresistible but I had to resist. Then at the next full meeting of the County Council I raised the matter of gifts as an agenda item, and referred to the cufflinks. I was fortunate in obtaining an unanimous vote that I should keep them, and I think that was the only exception made to the rule. I still wear them and enjoy them.

On a much larger scale on the Highways side was the intention to build an Inner Ring Road – around the City Centre area - to help the movement of traffic. The Labour party strongly objected as they did not wish to encourage traffic into the City Centre area – that was one reason why the M62 motorway stops some three or four miles from the City Centre, still causing dreadful bottlenecks. It seems that the Labour Party then could not reconcile the access of traffic with greater prosperity. Fortunately they changed later under different leadership, but this caused major problems at the time.

The inner ring road consisted of road widening generally, with some additions, and it was intended to go from the north, along the docks, and then turn left and left again to complete the ring, without disturbing the City Centre. I knew that the elections in 1981 were coming and that with a strong Conservative government at Westminster we were likely to lose to the Labour Party in local elections – that always seems to happen. In such a case the inner ring road would never happen. So I pushed it all I could. I held special meetings, but the Labour Party one day halted a Highways Committee meeting, which I was chairing, because they had obtained a Court injunction temporarily to stop any more progress, until the judge had decided whether or not we were following the correct procedures in the development.

I went to the Court at St George's Hall with my senior officers – before the new courts had opened – for the hearing. We won, and we could go ahead. The rush was on and the elections were looming. The contractors were McTay's. We in fact managed to get about half of it done before the elections interrupted and, indeed stopped, any further progress.

One Saturday lunchtime the telephone rang and it was a Chief Inspector Wilson of the Merseyside Police to ask if he could see me about the ring road. He came round, very apologetically, to say that they had received an anonymous letter from, he thought, a Liberal Councillor, although he could not be sure, alleging that I had been paid a bribe by McTay's to encourage the building of the road, and that I had used the bribe to buy ourselves a Rolls Royce Silver Shadow – not brand-new, I hasten to say. I told Mr Wilson to be at my office on the Monday morning, at our cashier's department. I also arranged that morning that the Chief Cashier was to show Mr Wilson all my personal documents, and anything else appertaining to me, that he wished to see. He was most grateful, went through everything, and was completely satisfied that I had used our own money for the car purchase – save that there was the sum of £1000 not accounted for. I could not think what it was and rang Sonia to see if she had any thoughts. As ever she came up with the answer, and asked if I had checked our building society accounts. I immediately did that and found that the 'missing' £1000 had been paid from there. I do not know who was more pleased, me or the Chief Inspector.

At the full Council meeting the following Thursday I raised this, gave a detailed explanation, and condemned the accusers of perfidy – that is a good word – and the air was completely cleared. But it shows the hazards which can suddenly come upon you in public life.

Most unexpected problems could arise and one hit me hard personally. One evening the cleaners at the County Headquarters had loaded the contents of masses of waste-paper baskets into dustbins, and then put them in one of the lifts to take them down for disposal. Somebody must have smoked – there was no ban in those days. Guess what? A bin caught fire, and so did the others. Smoke and dust filled the shaft and a number of the offices. I was telephoned at home urgently – it was, of course, out of office hours - and went to see the damage. I managed to get in despite the firemen doubting whether the smoke might be damaging to my lungs, and walked to the top – all 19 floors. The offices were alright other than smoke, the other lift shafts were pretty well alright, and the one where there had been the fire had suffered some damage. However they had to put all four out of action whilst repairs were carried out and this, they told me, would take about a month.

I was determined to continue to use my lovely office, even if it meant climbing 19 floors, but after a few days I gave that up and settled for a temporary office lower down. How delighted I was, a month later, when the lifts were working and I could go back to the top!

During this time I had quite a number of television broadcasts to do. The television people would meet me at the County Headquarters, or come to my office, on literally a few minutes' notice, complete with cameras, microphones, white umbrella to direct the light in the right direction, and setting up the camera. There was no time for preparation – they asked me the questions or opened the discussion, and off we went. I found them to be no problem as I sat at my office desk, pushed the file in front of me to one side, did the broadcast and then carried on with my work. I only remember one occasion when I got it wrong. The fact was that with a straightforward interview I could manage my answers by talking to the interviewer, oblivious of the cameras. The interviewer and I could have been having a friendly chat. But on one occasion I was asked to finish with the words 'I have a pride in Merseyside'. The interview went fine, but when it came to the prepared six words I stumbled over them. We had to repeat the interview and I think it was only on the fourth attempt I got it right. It is fortunate that the interview was recorded and not live. The moral of the story is that one is far better chatting naturally – or at least I am – than talking from a script. I would have been a dead loss in a Shakespearian play.

The office of the Leader of the Council was beautifully situated on the top floor – the 19th floor – of Metropolitan House, our Headquarters. There was a lovely view, no traffic noise, bright and attractive. There were now four functioning lifts in the centre of the fairly narrow but tall block giving easy access all round. I had on the walls – and I did not demand this but it was offered to me – pictures I really liked from the famous Walker Art Gallery. In addition my personal assistant had an office next to mine and everything was done for my convenience.

Anyway we got on with the Ring Road and put in hand contracts for the river-front stretch of it and a little more, but then came the time for elections. There was inevitably the great swing to Labour which we had anticipated, as there had previously been a great swing to the Tories, and our numbers in the County Council were reduced to 27 members out of the 99, with a number of Liberals in between. I became Leader of the Opposition. Among the first things Labour did was to cancel any further plans for the ring road on the political philosophy that Liverpool should be kept free of vehicles. I still cannot understand how they could think that a vehicle-free City could be a commercial or industrial success. Thus there was to be no more Inner Ring Road, and the approaches to the City Centre from the motorways were left as they were – fairly minor roads in many instances not intended to carry a great weight of traffic.

The City Centre was much more free of traffic than it would otherwise have been, and land which had been acquired for road improvement was sold off or used for other purposes. The great problem, which we foresaw and debated at length but which Labour strongly rejected, was that a great city cannot live without traffic movement. Most other great cities took action – Birmingham and Newcastle were good examples – but Liverpool remained strangled. Many years later, in better hands, the City Council endeavoured to do something about it but the Labour-controlled County Council, and I do not say this just because I am a Conservative, had made the position so difficult that the City did not prosper as it should have done for far longer than would otherwise have been the case. The added problem was that in due course the Metropolitan Counties were abolished, which left no overall highways authority, which had been one of the tasks of the County Council.

And so we were in opposition. This meant much less responsibility in running the County, but a lot to do in trying to get the controlling party to run the County properly. Nevertheless their majority was so great they could virtually steamroller anything they wished. Sometimes we could have a lighter moment. At one County Council meeting a Councillor Sylvia Renilson, Labour, as the Deputy Chairman of a committee, moved the minutes of that committee. Out of sheer bloody-mindedness I moved a reference back – that the items should be debated in detail. This debate would take place at the end of all the other council business.

The meeting started at 1.30 pm, and we got to the point of the reference back at about 7 pm – there had been a tea-break. During the whole of this time Sylvia had been making copious notes and whispering discussions with her colleagues. Then I was called on by the Chairman to move my reference back. I said that I had reconsidered the matter – I had not reconsidered it at all but was acting as I had originally intended - and said that I did not wish to proceed with my motion. Sylvia got up to reply, and to make her prepared speech, but the Chairman stopped her, as clearly she could not object to a proposal which had not been made. She had spent the whole afternoon preparing it and tried again and again, but he, quite rightly, said that there was nothing to which she could reply. She sat down livid and angry. That was the end of the Council meeting and we left the Chamber. In the cloakroom I was chatting to a couple of senior Labour councillors - our relationships in private were overall very friendly – and one of them said to me – 'Neville, you're a bastard………but you did it superbly!'.

At one Council meeting I observed that there were notices on the main highways leading into the County of Merseyside to say that it was a 'nuclear-free zone' – following a resolution of the Labour-controlled Council that such notices should be displayed. I observed that Russian bombers flying over with nuclear bombs were hardly likely to see the notices and one could not expect the pilot to say, in Russian of course, 'I am not going to bomb there – it is a nuclear-free zone'. I was appalled that money should be wasted on such rubbish.

The Labour Party went further than I expected – one of their members said that if I felt so strongly about it, I should go the United States and the Soviet Union and meet the Presidents and persuade them that we were indeed a nuclear-free zone. Before I could say a word this was seconded and passed with an amendment that a senior Labour councillor should come with me. I felt that this could be very interesting, although completely unproductive, and would indeed cost far less than the notices. I agreed. The following morning, as I was shaving – electrically in those days – the telephone rang and it was Roger Phillips of BBC Radio Merseyside, to ask if I would do an interview over the telephone there and then about these notices and the proposal which had been made. I agreed, and with my shaver – switched off – in one hand and the telephone in the other, we had our radio interview which was duly broadcast live as we spoke and repeated later on. Sonia was downstairs preparing breakfast listening to Radio Merseyside, when suddenly she heard me: How lucky that she did not run upstairs to ask me what was going on – it would have gone out over the air! Needless to say they later passed a resolution to cancel the visit.

There we some interesting personalities on the Merseyside County Council. Our Party Leader had been, at the outset Sir Kenneth

Thompson, Bart., who had received his Honour when he was kicked out of government on the 'night of the long knives' by Harold McMillan, the then Prime Minister. He coped well with polio which he had suffered as a child and which left him still quite disabled, but his mind was sharp. Being his Deputy was not easy. Another interesting personality was Bill Sefton – to become Lord Sefton of Garston (it is interesting that during the years of the County Council no Conservatives received any Honours whatsoever, but the other Parties did well) – who was the Labour Party and Council Leader from the beginning of the County Council until we won the next election in 1977. He used to speak as if he were addressing a Trade Union meeting – not that I have ever been to one – waving his arms and bending his knees to stress the points he tried to make.

Danny Dougherty, who worked in a Bank, had a thick 'scouse' (Liverpool) accent and a wonderful sense of humour. On one occasion he asked the Airport Chairman at Question Time, 'Is it correct that Aer Lingus (the Irish Airline) has outside toilets on its aircraft?' Another was Margaret Simey – Lady Simey - whose husband had been ennobled. She was very left-wing but stood her full height of nearly six feet and was as stern and humourless as any headmistress in literature. I remember asking her a question, and addressed her as Lady Simey. Being a good socialist, she interrupted me to say 'I should not be called Lady Simey, it should be Councillor Simey'. I replied by saying that I would never make the mistake of calling her a lady again. One of the Liberal Democrats was David Alton, with whom I disagreed but with whom I found it difficult to quarrel. He later went into Parliament and was elevated to the Lords.

During the years of the Merseyside County Council I think we proved it to be a very good organ of Local government. We had no show or pomp and circumstance, no uniformed attendants and no civic car. We just got on with the job and I would like to think we did it well. There were occasions where very strict steps were taken for breaches of the rules. There was one councillor – not of my party as it happens – who came to a Council Meeting as a passenger in the car of a colleague, and yet both claimed car expenses for the journey. It was only a matter of a few pounds but the one guilty of the 'sin', who had been in a very senior position as an elected member, had to retire from that post and go to the back benches. I am glad that they were so strict.

-oOo-

I must give the family a little look-in: Iain and Margaret's marriage has been a great success and now both of their children are married.

Nadine married Simon Caplan in the garden of the Holyland Hotel in Jerusalem in 1983. In the course of time they had three children and we are proud to have now two great-grandchildren. To jump ahead, things did not run to plan and in 2003 she divorced him.

-oOo-

Back to politics – can we ever get away from them? A great problem which the Government – a Conservative government – had at this time was the strength of the Metropolitan Counties. There were six in all plus greater London Council which was under the leadership of Ken Livingstone. The leaders of the seven of them used to meet every week to discuss policy, and they formed about one-third of the population of the country, so they were a powerful force. Locally, for example, they acquired large premises not only as the headquarters for the Labour Party, but the Party even had its own pub called 'The Flying Picket'. They were dangerous to the Conservative cause, but on the other hand in due course there was going to be a Labour Government with, inevitably, a much stronger presence of Conservatives in local government, and they could have waited.

However the Government – Margaret Thatcher was the Prime Minister - decided to get rid of the metropolitan counties, and the Secretary of State for the Environment, Patrick Jenkin, was put in charge. For reasons best known to him he, and his Minister of State, Lord Bellwin, used me as their contact 'on the ground', and so we met often. They asked my views, which were those of my colleagues as well as mine, and they appeared to be very interested. Indeed on one occasion at his request went to meet Irwin Bellwin in Leeds, where he lived, with a list of items which I, and my group in Merseyside, considered needed to be dealt with, with special care, before embarking on the termination of the Metropolitan Counties. He had himself been in local government and agreed, and said he would discuss it with Patrick.

As was always the case, they discussed it – and took not the slightest bit of notice of it. This went on all the way through, and whilst we locally could see where it was heading they took no notice. For example, when Merseyside County disappeared there would be five Metropolitan Boroughs in its place, but with Police and Fire to be under separate bodies run by nominees of these five councils. There were various bits and pieces like this which applied all over the country, whereas in the days of the County Council there was one Authority handling all major issues, with the metropolitan boroughs dealing with purely local matters.

The Government proposed that the Metropolitan Counties should disappear in April 1985. At the same time they were preparing to replace local rates with the poll tax. Again they wanted local opinion, and there was one meeting in Preston when the Secretary of State concerned, Cecil Parkinson, came up to discuss it with Conservative leaders. He listened, or said he listened, to all we said. We were all worried about the type of tax, its impact on local people and facilities, the local reaction and the damage it could cause.

It was due to come in, so far as I recall, in April 1986, a year after the Metropolitan Counties disappeared. However there were delays in organizing the abolition of the counties, as it had proved to be a far more difficult and complicated task than they had anticipated. It was decided to delay it for a year.

Clearly this was discussed at the regular meetings between Ken Livingstone and his Labour leaders, and the upshot was that all the Metropolitan Counties decided to spend, spend and spend, so that by the time their abolition came they had no reserves. I clearly remember a new library being built locally with a large hall attached, and this was happening all over the country.

The abolition of the Metropolitan Counties, then, coincided with the introduction of the poll tax. There was one problem, however, which the government had managed not to see, and that was that the new Metropolitan Borough Councils would have no reserves of cash, having spent every penny they had, and so local taxes – now the poll tax – would have to be higher than it would otherwise have been. The rate throughout the country was overall so high that there was uproar and the tax lasted for, I think, just one year, or it may have been two. But this did a lot of damage to the Conservative Government and again they had played right into Labour's hands. The tax introduced to replace poll tax was called Council Tax, which was on a better basis, and the shock of the increase had already been taken up, and so it was accepted – albeit reluctantly - by the majority of the population.

When the Metropolitan Counties were destined to finish on this further reorganization of local government I felt that I would have a little more time on my hands to work in the office. I was doing mostly commercial work by this time, as gradually I had been able to rid myself of such mundane things as divorce, crime, accident cases and 'trippers'. These were cases where somebody tripped over a pavement and claimed from the City Council. For reasons I have never been able to fathom the local authorities always paid up without a fight and I am sure that because the claimants had 'won' damages from them comparatively easily, their friends were encouraged to trip over the same 'trip'. There was one uneven pavement outside one of my offices which brought a 'tripper' in. He was successful. I think there followed about a dozen more who 'tripped' over the same paving stone before the local authority ultimately repaired it.

I had been negotiating a merger with another firm, the two senior partners of which had been articled to me and so were, in effect, trained by me, and so I could not criticise their skills. We had six offices and they had six as well, so it would have been a twelve-office firm. I was not keen to be involved in the administration of so many offices, and knew that as senior partner I would be very heavily tied up. So I negotiated a package whereby I was to be the Consultant to the firm – full time or more of course – but would have no responsibility for the running of the offices. My requirement was that I should be properly paid as if I had been a senior partner and this was agreed.

It worked well. I was still busy with my political life in the final months of the Metropolitan Counties but was still able to be a major earner in the practice by dint of hard work and putting in the hours. At last I had a complete freedom of choice as to the work I did, and so I moved further away from the humdrum and the more repetitive work to my preferred commercial work. This consisted among other things of company takeovers, substantial leases, and large property deals. The work was in many ways harder, one had to get every detail right – but then that always applied to all branches of the law – but there was usually a lot more at stake. We were working in big figures.

-oOo-

Chapter 12
Back To The True Blues

It was in 1986, not long after the merger, that I was approached to be the Chairman of the Crosby Conservative Association. I decided to accept as I had seen, from previous years, that it had not been too onerous a job, but would still have some interest and keep me in touch with the political scene. On being elected – and it was a contested election (I cannot remember ever being appointed to anything political without a contest, but fortunately I had won each time) - I went to our Headquarters to cement my relationship with the Conservative Agent. Hers was really a job that covered everything from being the typist to the chief executive, all the other jobs being done by volunteers. My Agent was Vanessa Wilson, a youngish lady with a good brain and a good right hand to have.

One of the first things I did was to investigate the financial position of the Association. I found – I had not known this before – that we were supposed to give a quota of about £5000 each year, a lot of money then, to Conservative Central Office, but we had never been able to give anything more than a few hundred pounds. My first problem, then, was to raise money, and at the same time to raise political interest.

I had an idea: I thought that if we could get some government high flyer, or some cabinet minister, to come, we might raise a few pounds and enliven interest in the Association and the Party. Fortunately I had made good contacts with Conservative Central Office over the years, and so I decided to fly high. I contacted Nigel Lawson, then Chancellor of the Exchequer, and one of the most senior members of the government, to see if he would come up to Crosby for a function. After some correspondence and telephone calls I persuaded him, although an extremely busy man, to come up for a luncheon.

The next question was the venue, because I knew that he was a big attraction and a big place was needed. I approached the president of the Waterloo Rugby Club, the Club itself being pretty prestigious, and he agreed to provide a large function room there with minimum or no charge. Then came the question of catering. Vanessa during this time had stood by feeling sure that all that I planned was impossible – and at times I felt that she was probably right – but how were we to cover the cost of catering, and how much would people pay to come?

I hit on an idea, and with this Vanessa thought that I was completely mad. The idea was that the Conservative ladies would cater it, and we would have to find a number of volunteers for that as it could not be any sort of lunch, and the bombshell came when I told Vanessa that I had decided that the function would be free. So far as I recall I had a committee, but I felt that this was far too important to be delayed by committee approval at each stage – or at all! After all, what is democracy?

I decided to implement my idea by personally heading and tailing seven hundred letters of invitation. I had one hundred and ten affirmative replies, and so we were in business. Clearly there was reason to believe that it could be an interesting meeting and that it would raise the status of the Association, but the food still had to be paid for, as had the paper, postages, notices, advertisements, and all the other extras which always add up in these functions.

Nigel Lawson duly turned up on a lovely sunny day. I had the press there to squeeze every bit of publicity out of it. I was talking to Lawson beforehand as he had always seemed, on radio and television, to be a very interesting person. In fact I am afraid that I found him to be rather aloof, but that did not matter – the fact was the Chancellor of the Exchequer was there to speak.

Nigel Lawson spoke adequately well and the public enjoyed it. I thanked him and included my thanks to the guests. I continued, 'This is, of course, a free lunch. No demands will be made on your pockets. Nevertheless any additional donations would of course be very welcome – and I should mention that we have bouncers at each exit!'. The guests all had envelopes on their tables in which to put any donation which they might choose to give. The 'bouncers' never had to bounce. When we added it all up afterwards we had received as clear profit from our free lunch the sum of £3000 – a lot of money at that time.

That set the pattern for me. If we could do it with Nigel Lawson we could do it with others. The Association members were now most enthusiastic, I had as many helpers as I could want, and Vanessa really came up trumps and did all that was needed.

Thereafter I had a number of senior members of the government as the guests of the Association. There was at that time a popular programme on television known as 'The Morecambe and Wise Show', in the course of which many senior personalities, even those in government, used to go along and join in one of the shows. My luncheons and dinners became known as the equivalent of Morecambe and Wise, to the extent that if a Cabinet Minister had not been one of my guests, he would have been regarded as a failure!

I had a whole pile of them. One guest was Chris Patten who became the last Governor of Hong Kong and was later a European Commissioner and then Chancellor of Oxford University. Whilst in our house before going to meetings Chris sat in our new 'parrot chair', a chair rather like a cage and suspended from a bracket on an iron stand. We had a job to move him out of it, he was so comfortable there! We were twice in Hong Kong when he was in office as Governor and had the pleasure of being entertained for breakfast the first time, and drinks the second time, at Government House. He and his wife were most helpful and delightful company – indeed my hobby was to make serious video documentaries, and he was good enough to allow me to have a formal interview with him which would have been good enough for BBC 2. I would mention that when, some time later, Hong Kong reverted to China and Chris's job was done, and Government House was vacated, the Chinese refused to use it for anything at all because of 'fung chu' – the shape, position or the style of the building was, they considered, unlucky.

Another favourite was Denis Thatcher, the husband of the Prime Minister. He stayed with us and you could not have had a nicer or more considerate guest. He was a perfect gentleman, and, in fact, more than that, he was a very decent and good person. The tale ran that he always drank pink gins, and so when we got back home after a couple of functions I gave him one. He hardly had a sip all evening, and the tales about him never being seen without a drink in his hand were nonsense.

He came by train and I met him at Lime Street Station, Liverpool. He had no escort and no security. A police inspector came to the station as a matter of courtesy to say 'hello' and then he left and then Denis and I went off home. When he left again the next day there was no security, even when someone on the station came up and asked 'Aren't you Denis Thatcher?'. Denis carried it off perfectly. He attended two functions the evening he was with us, made good speeches and went a bomb with everybody. He was one of the easiest guests I had.

The complete contrary to that informality, and it was not his fault but the fault of his position in government, was when George Younger, the Defence Secretary, was here. He had a constant armed guard. The house was checked out in the morning with sniffer dogs, there were police outside whilst he was inside, and when we changed to go out for a dinner he changed in one room, the leading security man, gun and all, changed in the spare room, the next security man put on his black tie in the loo.

Similar to this was Douglas Hurd, the then Home Secretary, and this was the time of the Irish troubles. He turned up in a Land Rover with police cars in front and behind, as he drove up to a meeting I had arranged at Aintree Racecourse. Nobody – not even me – was allowed to park near to him. He had always struck me as fairly dull and staid, but he was excellent company, with a very good sense of humour, and the sort of person you want to meet again.

Another interesting and very pleasant person was Leon Britten, then a European Commissioner. There was no affectation about him at all. He spoke and mixed so very well and that was another successful function. Indeed there were quite a few more and there is no need to list them all, but all my guests behaved impeccably – bar one, who was particularly conceited and arrived late to boot, but it would be cavalier of me to name him. I will just mention however that at that time he was the Secretary of State for the Environment, and he lost his way coming here.

Angela Rumbold was Secretary of State for Education and Science, and again she was another easy and very welcome guest. Then there was Cecil Parkinson, Energy Secretary. All were very pleasant to deal with and did all I asked of them except for one. And that one was Geoffrey Archer. He duly came up, and I was to meet him at the Southport Constituency Headquarters. When I arrived in the car with my agent the Southport agent came out and asked for the cricket test-match scores from the radio as Archer wanted them. We went back to the car to check the position but it was the interval and there were no scores available – just music. We went in to meet the Southport Chairman and Archer, and the agent told him that he could not give him the scores, and explained why. 'You twerp', said Archer, and the turned to us ' Don't you think he's a twerp'? and the man was there, to listen to that!

We went on our way. Vanessa was driving and I was at the back with Archer and I told him the programme for the evening. I told him that at each of the two planned events I would make a speech of introduction and then he would speak. He said 'Oh, I do hope that you will not go on too long in your speech. I have listened to 204 Conservative chairmen in the last two years and they bore me to tears'.

I replied, 'That is a strange coincidence: You are my 204th guest, and I have been dreading your speech all week because I get so tired of these speeches. I hope that it won't be as bad as I fear'. After that he almost behaved himself!

We held our meetings at the Conservative Clubs and headquarters in the various parts of the constituency and there was tremendous enthusiasm. It was at that time the second largest constituency in the country, with some 80,000 people residing in it. By the time my three years were up we had paid the full quota to Conservative Central Office each year and in addition there was £25,000 sitting in the bank – quite a sum of money in those days. I was asked to stay on for another three years, but the time to go is when things are going well, so I gracefully retired and left it to my successors to increase or decrease the money in hand.

During all these years everything was made possible by the fact that Sonia mucked in superbly in everything. She never pushed herself but was always ready and willing to do whatever was asked and whatever public duties were required. She gave house-room to cabinet ministers – indeed she almost became a boarding-house keeper - catered for distinguished visitors, and made everything appear to be so easy when she was, after all, combining this with her very busy medical practice. Not only this, but she made sure that I was so well looked after and ready for anything that was required of me. She gave speeches when she needed to, very often impromptu – in fact I was, and still am, very proud of her and tremendously grateful. Without her backing life would have been infinitely more difficult, if not impossible. I realised then, as I always do, how tremendously clever I had been in the past – my brilliance was to propose to her before anybody else had the opportunity.

-oOo-

Chapter 13
The Law Takes Over Again

We were now up to 1989, and I had a bit more time to devote to the office. I had merged Goldrein & Co with Levy Deacon and Green in 1986, I had an excellent room in our main office which was in the Liverpool City Centre. There were twenty offices by now. At the outset we had six offices each which, if my mathematics are correct, came to twelve. This was gradually extended and the main office, where I worked, was moved to Harrington Street.

On the merger the first thing to be decided was the name, and it was amazing how much argument there was about that. However I suggested the simple solution of alphabetical order, and so the new firm was called Deacon Goldrein Green. With such a large outfit, and I was getting a little older, I was not anxious to have too much, or any, capital tied up in the firm. My own firm had no overdraft and I had more or less complete control as the other partners left it to me to a great extent. Here, with twelve partners, and later twenty partners, it was not going to be so easy.   In the other firm the partners had always had their own homes given as security for the practice overdraft, and I did not intend to be part of that.   And so I made a suggestion, which was accepted, that I should have the best private office in the firm, that my salary would be about that of the senior partners, that I would have no personal responsibility, and that I should be a consultant and not a partner.

All this was agreed, which left me to do the work I enjoyed most. I had, when I first put my own plate up, taken all comers from street assaults to conveyancing to dock accidents. Now I could choose and, as I have said, I specialised in commercial work. I still found myself working, probably from force of habit apart from pressure of work, from about eight in the morning until about six in the evening but if, at any time, I felt like a slightly longer holiday, I could take one.

Not very long after we got going with the twelve offices we were approached by a solicitor who had eight offices in the Wirral and he suggested a further merger. This was done, giving us twenty offices, and that brought it up to twenty partners, and a staff of over two hundred – a little more than the 'none' I had started with!   I was invited to partners' meetings to advise but, of course, with no vote. That worked well but I noticed that gradually the invitations to me to attend partners' meeting became fewer and fewer. I did not mind, but I realised that they had bitten off a lot, and the financial state was not as good as it had been – indeed it was bound to get worse before it could get better. I felt, and feel, that they preferred me not to be at meetings as I am a cautious person, I never do or try to do more than can be achieved, and have no streak of the gambler. That did not fit in with their expansionist plans. The position was made even more difficult as about this time Minimum Scale Fees for conveyancing were discontinued by the Law Society and so conveyancing, which had been most profitable, ceased to be so, and this affected particularly the new Wirral offices which were nearly all conveyancing-orientated. All this confirmed to me how right I had been to decide to be a consultant and not a partner. The firm prospered but I had no personal liability.

In 1990 we decided to have a holiday in South Africa. We first went to Zimbabwe, which had until not long before been Rhodesia, and went first to Harare, the capital. We were fortunately there before Mugabe completely ruined the country. The hotel was good, service good, and the climate and countryside were delightful. The only problem was that the local traders found was that street names kept changing as government ministers wished to name the roads after themselves. That was alright in itself but the various traders and professionals had to change their notepaper so often to keep up with the street-name changes.

We went out on some early-morning safaris in a Land Rover and saw the big game really close up, including lions only a few feet away. We had to get up early for these as the wild life goes for a rest when it gets warmer – at about seven in the morning. I had learned this in Somalia.

From there we went to the Victoria Falls and flew over them in a light aircraft. Sonia was, I am sure rightly, very worried as the pilot was rotund and red faced and obviously a drinker. There was no co-pilot, but Sonia was concerned in case he had a heart-attack. Fortunately this did not occur then – but it did some time later.

Then we flew via Johannesburg to Durban, a lovely city and stayed at a beautiful Indian hotel. But near there we saw some of the camps where the poor blacks lived and were absolutely horrified whilst being tremendously impressed at the same time as to the way they managed to live and be clean and cheerful in such conditions.

We took the famous 'Garden Route' by bus to Capetown via two African townships, Tranksei and Siskei. Capetown was a beautiful city and the relationship between black and white was easing, but 'apartheid' was still very much there. Table Mountain was one of the most beautiful sights we had seen, and we took the funicular railway to the top. We had the privilege, too, of going to the houses of parliament and had personal discussions with the leaders of the three main parties – ranging from one which really desired an end to apartheid – separation of whites and blacks – to one who considered that apartheid was essential and the blacks were far better being treated as inferior citizens. Physically as to the country, and politically, the whole time there was fascinating. It would be particularly interesting to return and see what differences there are today.

In 1991 my very lovely mother-in-law, who had been fine and up and running since I had known her, became ill and had to go to hospital. She was 95 and very game, and she even managed to get well enough to get out of hospital. However she was getting weaker and soon after her return she died peacefully. The wonderful part was that she was only really unwell for about two weeks. Sonia, who adored her mother, quite rightly, coped as she always does.

My mother-in-law had always hoped that one day I would get an honour for what I had done in my public and political life, but that was something never in my sights as not being within the bounds of possibility. The sad thing is that just a few months after she died I received a letter to say that I would receive a C.B.E. - or, to be more pompous, would be appointed a Commander of the Order of the British Empire. There are only 230 appointed in any one year. I was astonished as it is not only an honour, but a very good one at that. If I had got an O.B.E. (400 in any one year) or even an M.B.E. (700), I would have been pleased but the one I was to get was really something special. The letter arrived whilst we were on holiday and had been lying about inside our letterbox for over a week before I saw it. I was horrified in case they changed their minds in view of the non-reply from me, so I quickly said 'yes' and dashed out to post the letter. I was clearly told that the whole thing was entirely confidential and that no mention of it should be made to anyone, and so we kept our mouths tightly shut. We did not even tell Iain and Nadine until the evening before the newspapers appeared on the occasion of the Queen's Official Birthday with the lists of honours being granted.

Then the congratulations came pouring in and my firm's letterheads were changed as the firm was very proud to display it. Of course every congratulation had to have a reply, and I did these individually as I preferred not to send a printed card of thanks to people who had been so kind as to write.

There was a fair amount of documentation to lead up to it and we were allowed to take Iain with us – only children, but Margaret, Iain's wife, could not be there as she was not our child. Nadine was away in Israel. I had one query and so I telephoned the Palace, and to my amazement a very cockney voice answered 'Buckin'ham Palace'. I asked to be put through to someone dealing with the minutiae of the investiture. I was immediately put through to a voice at the other end which one would have expected in the first place from such a source, the 'right' voice! He was most helpful and dealt with my queries. Then I had to wait for the official summons to tell me on what day the Investiture would be held. There are, I think, three investitures, so that if you will be away for one you can always manage to be there for one of the others.

We spent the night before at the Grosvenor House Hotel, deciding to do it in style, and on the day of the Investiture we turned up at Buckingham Palace, drove in through the gates and parked in the inner courtyard. Then we entered the Palace and the fun started.

We walked in – through the front door – and Sonia and Iain were duly shown to the Ballroom where the ceremony was to take place, and I decided before I did anything else to follow my very practical maxim – 'a wise man when he can and a fool when he must' – and went to the loo. Standing next to me was Iain, who had been trained, after all, by me and his comment was: 'Well, Dad, this is the great leveller'.

We then parted and I went up the Grand Staircase, and it is grand. On each step, inside the banister of this curved stairway, was a member of the Household Cavalry, with cuirass, sword, plumed helmet – the full glory. And there was not a movement. I wondered for a moment if they were real or wax, and then decided that they were indeed real, and I felt a great pride in our whole system in this country, and this epitomised it. One had to remember, too that these guardsmen were not only a wonderful part of the ceremonial, but among the best soldiers in the country too.

As I walked up the stairs I said to myself, 'Here am I, first generation English–born from an Eastern European Jewish family, walking up the Grand Staircase of Buckingham Palace'. It was hardly credible. I asked Sonia afterwards what she was thinking as she was sitting in the Ballroom, she having heard from Iain that I was to be walking up that staircase. She had, at the moment I thought it, had the identical thought. This has happened many times but not usually in such prestigious places.

Once up there those who were to receive the C.B.E. were separated from the O.B.E.s and M.B.E.s, as those to be honoured with these were to receive medals to be pinned on, and they had to put a special clip on their chests – jacket or dress - to make it easier for the Queen to put it on rather than that she should have to mess about pinning it on. Mine was a neck decoration and so a slightly different procedure was to be followed, with the added advantage that there were far fewer of us as not so many C.B.E.s are granted. An officer of the Guards in blue patrol dress uniform came to explain to us the detailed procedure. He had a beautiful fruity voice – indeed he could not have been anything other than a fairly senior Guards' officer. His instructions were clear and brief, given with a good sense of humour, although I am sure that the jokes had been the same for generations.

Having dealt with that we were marshalled in a line with the more senior ones in the front of the line, followed by the less senior orders, and so I was pleased to be in the first batch after the knights. Then we were very politely guided towards the Ballroom, and through the corridors of the Palace we walked. There were lovely paintings on the walls, worth a queen's ransom, and the whole thing was carried out to perfection.

Then we came to a halt whilst those few in front were invested. They were the Knights who were, of course, senior to us, and then forward we went. The corridor ended and on our right was the wide entrance, through which we would pass into the Ballroom itself. I remember one or two having their names called and going forward, and then it was going to be me. A most courteous usher asked me most politely, 'Are you nervous, sir?'. I replied, with all honesty, 'Not in the least – should I be?'.

Then I heard the Lord chamberlain call out 'Commanders of the Order of the British Empire.   Mr Neville Clive Goldrein'.   I must confess that I derived a lot of pleasure from the fact that with a name like that there was no doubt that I was Jewish, and I was very proud of that fact. I have always appreciated how fortunate, or well-judged, it was that my parents had come to England – they could have gone anywhere in the world, including most European countries, and had they gone elsewhere there is little doubt that none of us would have survived. Indeed we owe our lives to the United Kingdom. Furthermore there is, I think, nowhere in the world where they have such systems of rewards and which are carried out with such fantastic ceremony, yet which are in no way intimidating.

And so here I was, walking across the front of the assembled audience, with a broad dais on my left, with officers and other ranks of the Brigade of Guards and the Ghurkha Regiments standing there, and then I was asked to pause for a moment by another usher whilst the recipient in front of me walked off.

Then my moment had come: I was asked then to move forward, I came in front of the Queen, and turned left to face her. Then I walked some three or four paces forward so that I was right in front of her and bowed. She shook hands. She had the ribbon and insignia in her hands – having had it passed to her by an officer who had to get everything absolutely in order - and I leaned forward, as I had been instructed, so that she could put it round my neck.

Then we had a little chat. To my pleasant surprise she asked me about my work in Merseyside and seemed to be aware of the reasons for the honour she was bestowing. Clearly there must have been a whisper in her ear just before I came up, but she did it very well.

As I have modestly mentioned, I had met the Queen a few times before but on this day she really excelled herself. Then she held out her hand

and we shook hands and I stepped back three or four paces, bowed again, turned right and strolled off.

Immediately I turned the corner there was another usher who took off my new C.B.E., removed the ribbon, replaced it with a very narrow ribbon, put it in a special case, and handed it to me and ushered me back to the 'audience' area in the ballroom. It is interesting that the C.B.E., being a neck decoration, is worn high on the neck with a very narrow ribbon. But the Queen would not have been able to put that on and clip it at the back, which would have meant my turning with my back to her. So the system is that she had been handed the medal on a long and wide ribbon so that she can put it on over my head, but once that is done the wide ribbon is never used again and, when I have had opportunities to wear the decoration since then, it is always worn with the small ribbon and worn high up on the neck.

From there I went to the Ballroom but I could not sit with Sonia and Iain, as I was much further back as were all the other recipients, and we sat through the remaining honours. The Investiture was due to last for an hour and it lasted for an hour – precisely. Then the Queen smiled and waved, and left the dais. During the whole of this procedure, from start to finish, a small group of musicians from the Guards' band was playing in the gallery at the opposite end of the Ballroom from the Queen.

Then we left and went outside, collecting my grey topper on the way. There were no refreshments – not even a glass of water. But outside there was a number of photographers and, like everybody else, Sonia and I had our photo taken with me holding my 'gong' in its case, open for all to see. We had to pay for that of course, but not on the spot as otherwise it would have looked far too commercial. In addition apparently there are four concealed video cameras in the Ballroom, and afterwards one can buy the tape which I did at the exorbitant price of £130, very expensive in the money of that time. It runs for about twenty minutes, and it takes in all the preparations and the preliminary talk and procession and, of course, a close-up of the person being invested – in this case, me!

It is not a tape made just for our investiture on that day, and it showed various people who had been there before, and so no doubt people being invested after me may well have seen me on their tape. But it does become personal for the investiture itself, as it shows me walking up, being 'done', chatting to the Queen, and walking away. In fact it was worth every penny, or pound, of the exorbitant sum I paid for it. From there we went to lunch at the Grosvenor House with Iain to celebrate and compare notes.

-oOo-

Chapter 14
Seeing The World

It was during this period that Sonia and I decided to do what we had always wanted to do – to go round the world, and we decided to do this in 1992. We worked out that it would take five weeks, but the partners were prepared to accept this, although Sonia had to pay for expensive locums during that period. We ascertained that if you fly one way only and use not more than two airlines the fares were surprisingly reasonable, and we were to travel Business Class with such distances involved. We decided to fly west to make the days longer and with less jet-lag – although on the way whilst we gained an hour each day, we suddenly lost a whole day. Fortunately it was not a birthday!

We went first to Los Angeles, then Hawaii, where we saw Pearl Harbour. It was not only sad to see it, but also to see so many Japanese tourists looking at the sunken ships – the very ships they had sunk. It was as if they were there to look at what they had achieved. There was one lighter side: When we were due to leave for the airport the taxi which had been booked for us in England was not there, and so we complained to management and stressed the urgency. They decided to put things right by arranging, themselves, for another car to take us.

When we went out, to our amazement, we saw a 'stretched limo', but really stretched: White, with darkened windows, a real gangster chief's means of transportation. Inside was a seat across the back, where we sat, a long table with seats round it, a cocktail cabinet (which we did not use) and a television. We decided that, when we got home, we would stick to the car we already had!

From there we went to Fiji. The royal guards wore 'skirts' – their version, I suppose, of the Scottish kilt. The people were most hospitable and the country, whilst poor, was really lovely. The next stop was New Zealand. We landed at Auckland which was a delightful city, although it seemed to 'go to bed' at about six in the evening, rather like a small English provincial town, and we visited Roturua nearby with its most impressive steam geysers, rather like the ones you see in Iceland. Then we flew down to Christchurch. On the flight from Auckland to Christchurch in a Boeing 737 the captain allowed me to sit on the flight deck, and it was fascinating to see how a jet came down, waiting for an aeroplane on the ground to take off – and then another – and then we landed on the same runway. This was a lovely city, very like Cambridge, with punts on the river and the men manning them wearing straw boaters. We went to a concert in the open air in the evening. The area was lovely, the orchestra was excellent and as the finale they played Tchaikovsky's 1812. Then at the crucial moment, as they let off the fireworks, it started to rain with the sort of rain we never see, fortunately, in this country. We had wondered why the hotel had provided us with umbrellas as we left for the concert when it was such a lovely evening, and now we knew. It made an English thunderstorm seem like a light shower.

From Christchurch we took a train across to Greystones on the west coast – a small industrial area and not much to see, but it was worth it for the train ride. Then we flew to Australia. In Australia we landed in Sydney. We wanted to see the Barrier Reef. Before going there Sonia and I were in a shop selling, among other things, sea-sick tablets. I said that we did not need those and I wondered why they offered them for sale. The sea was like a lake and the weather was beautiful. The next day we embarked on a large catamaran and off we went, in a perfectly smooth sea, and I told Sonia how wrong she was to buy the sea-sick tablets. We stopped off at an island to take on more passengers, and then off we went off again – and so did the sea! I have never travelled on such rough waters. It was impossible even to move from one chair to another. The restaurant was empty. At last we got to the Reef. Having gone as far as that I had to do what I had always wanted to do, and that was to snorkel and look more closely at the reef. We managed to get off the boat onto a large moored raft, which was not quite as susceptible to the rough waters as had been the catamaran but still rough enough, and then I managed to strip down to my trunks. I put on my snorkel and flippers and in I went. One thing about swimming is that you are not sea-sick, but the problem was that looking down at the reef, it kept moving away into the distance and then being a yard or so beneath me – the water was so rough that I went up and down with it to that extent.

Eventually I got out and there was the dreadful prospect of the journey back. Sonia asked the captain of the catamoran if the weather would be as bad as when we came, and he told us that it would be worse. At that moment a helicopter arrived and dropped some people off on a neighbouring raft. We asked if we could travel on it on the way back to avoid the horrors of another boat journey, and fortunately there were two seats left. I forget how we got from our raft to the other one where the 'chopper' had landed, but I clearly recall the relief as the chopper took off and the ride was as smooth as on a motorway, whilst the ocean below was raging. It cost us a few pounds but money has never been better spent.

Then we went back to Sydney to stay there for a few days. We thought it was a great and most attractive city. There were beaches, markets, seafront walks, shops, parks and British letter-boxes. We felt very much at home. The concert in the Opera House was excellent, although apparently because they had overrun their budget when building it they had decided to put in as many seats as possible. This meant that there was no central gangway. The result was that at the interval, and we were sitting near to the centre, it took us some time to get to the gangway. Then it was a very long walk to the loo, and a longer queue for the ladies. We got back to the concert just in the nick of time, as had we been any later we would have disturbed the whole row getting back to our seats. During the next few days we went to the beaches, took boat rides across the bay, walked along King's Cross, and visited the local street market. The weather was perfect and the people warm and friendly. The whole atmosphere was very English. Indeed on the final leg of our flight back we asked each other where we should live were we not in England. We thought first of Christchurch which was so delightful, but then thought that such a small town would be a long way from anywhere and perhaps a little lacking in culture. So we settled for Sydney.

The final leg was to Kuala Lumpur, Malaysia's capital city. We had been there before but it was worth it again, if only to see the Malaysian spelling with English characters – and so there was no difficulty in finding a 'Teksi'. The river and river buses and 'teksis' were fascinating and the railway station looks like a stately home or grand museum. It was clearly built when the British had enough money in the colonies to use it for such delights. As we drove in a taxi to see one of the sights I felt that the taxi – sorry, teksi – driver – was taking us 'for a ride'. So I asked Sonia, 'Is he going the right way?', as if she knew any better than I did. She calmly answered in the affirmative and indeed he had taken us the right way, but that may be because the question had kept him on his toes.

-oOo-

Chapter 15
Retirement – Or Was It?

As you will remember, Sonia had her surgery in her parents' house which she had arranged when they came to Merseyside so that she could keep an eye on them. When her Mother died she carried on in practice – she could not just cut it off at the drop of a hat – but clearly the house was not the same, however busy she was. Later in the year she had done a morning surgery and after the staff had gone, and she was in the house on her own, she heard a noise downstairs like a door closing and thought that 'it must be Mummy'. She started to go down to see her when, of course, she realised with great pain that there was no Mummy. She is a tremendously brave and, indeed, is a very wonderful person – as you may have gathered - but she mentioned it to me when I got home, not for sympathy but just to tell me about her day. I realised that it must have been very hard for her to carry on as long as she had – it had been some months – and I asked her why she did not retire. She had worked hard for years, was adored by her patients, but the time had come, I felt, for her to retire and rest and not put herself in the position that she had faced that morning.

She duly retired and kept pretty busy tidying things up, organizing things, and starting a new way of life and doing some locums for other doctors. She was asked by one doctor if she would work four days a week for him on a regular basis at a reasonable salary, but I felt that she had worked hard and long for long enough, and it would hardly be retiring to work again almost full time, so she rejected the offer but she still undertook regular locums until 2009. She almost had a full-time job answering all the letters from literally hundreds of grateful patients. Indeed years – many years – later we could – and indeed can - not walk round the local Sainsburys or Crosby generally without people stopping us to say what a wonderful doctor Sonia had been and how much they missed her, and they are still doing this and long may it continue. I love every moment of it.

Then I thought a thought. We had married to be together, and here was the opportunity for us to do just that. So I decided to retire and told my partners that this was what I intended to do, and why. They were helpful and in the summer of 1992 I did that, with a pleasant farewell party in the office and all the nice things were said.

And there we were, together at last, and our time was ours. But I wondered whether or not I would miss the professional life I had led and enjoyed for so long. On the other hand we did not want to become vegetables, which is always a danger on retirement, and decided to keep busy, but doing as much as we possibly could together. A good friend of ours, Bernard Jackson, was Professor of Law at Liverpool University, and we were with him socially one evening when he very kindly invited us to attend some of his lectures at the University Law School. And so for two years we attended his lectures two days a week, on Roman Law, Law Linguistics and Psychology and Biblical Law – that was part of a Ph.D. Course.

We enjoyed every moment of it. Bernard was a good lecturer, a very good personality and the subjects were stimulating. There was one fascinating lecture in the 'Law Linguistics and Psychology' lectures which dealt with jury trial. With the permission of the judge in a Crown Court in Liverpool there had been a representative of Granada

Television taking shorthand notes of every word of the trials – there were five in all – and in all five, again with the permission of the judge, there was a 'dummy jury' in court. When it was all over the television company re-enacted each case, word for word, and then at the lectures we watched selected and particularly relevant parts of the trials.

We could also go into the dummy jury's jury room and listen to their deliberations, something neither of us could ever had done for real because doctors and lawyers were not then eligible - although they are now. In the film of the dummy jury room there was an older chap – he was a taxi driver – who started off by saying that he was older than most of the others and he would be chairman. They agreed – it would have been rather embarrassing to do otherwise. Then during their deliberations he got into an argument with a woman who was a trade union convener. After a time he said that he was not prepared to listen to her any more and her opinion was of no interest to him. Then a younger couple made their observations, but he pointed out that they were young and it was better if the matter was left to the older and more mature members.

Then one of the 'jurors' said that, as there were two charges against the defendant, why did they not find him guilty of one and acquit on the other. 'Which one?' asked the self-appointed foreman, and the reply was, 'It doesn't really matter'. Ultimately this strange collection came to a decision as to guilt or innocence and decided on their verdict.

What struck me then, as it does now, as being remarkable, is that in four and a half of the five cases the dummy juries agreed with the real juries. One wonders what happens behind closed doors with a real jury. I have always admired the system and still do, but I would dearly love to eavesdrop on a real jury. Perhaps they are all like the one we saw. As it happens after I retired I was summoned to sit on a jury as lawyers and doctors were by then no longer exempt, but unfortunately I was too old – I think the top age is 70 – and so I shall never know.

We attended the lectures most conscientiously for two years and then found that we had accumulated so many other commitments that we had to discontinue. But we shall always be grateful to Bernard Jackson for introducing us to retirement in that way. In the course of those lectures, too, we attended a special lecture arranged by Bernard, the lecturer being Justice Gabriel Bach of the Israeli Supreme Court, who addressed a meeting of students. In his younger days Gabriel Bach was assistant prosecutor in the Eichmann trial. Bernard then asked us, and Gabriel Bach, to dinner at his home. We have remained friends of the Bachs ever since and when in Jerusalem we have dinner or evenings – or both – together.

The even greater benefit was that we had not missed our previous careers at all. We were lucky in that we had enjoyed what we had done all our working lives: Sonia really enjoyed her medicine, and the gratitude of her patients showed that. I looked back, and still do, on my life as a solicitor and found it very stimulating and challenging, particularly managing to build up a 'nothing' one-man show into a substantial practice. Being a judge had been exciting, stimulating and very satisfying, and the political side was, as the title of this book suggests, far too serious to be taken seriously, and that may be why I have enjoyed it so much. But retirement was just as good – indeed better because we could be together most of the time and, after all, we married to be together.

We are up to 1994, and one thing that happened that year is that I was approached and asked if I would be the Chairman of the Trustees of a new trust to be founded to run the Liverpool Royal Court Theatre. This theatre was built just before World War II and many very famous actors and actresses had appeared there. It was, and is, acoustically perfect, and there are no pillars or other obstructions whatsoever between the stage and the audience. I had remembered it many years before and it had always impressed me. During the days of the County Council it was decided that the County should take over one of the Liverpool Theatres, and the choice was between the Empire and the Royal Court. I had always preferred the Royal Court, and we went to see both theatres. The problem with the Royal Court at that time was that it was very dilapidated and there was an ugly and large projection box set at the back of the stalls which ruined that part of the theatre. And so we decided, reluctantly so far as I was concerned, to take the Empire. We held that until the County Council died, and I was a director during the whole of that period, and so I got to know the theatre well.

However here was my chance to get back to my beloved Royal Court and without even having a look at it I agreed. The chief executive was Simon Geddes, about six feet six tall, and left me feeling that I should be on a step-ladder to talk to him, but he was a delightful fellow and wonderful to work with. So I went, with Simon, to have a look at my new commitment. I was horrified! The theatre was more like a dilapidated slum than a theatre, the proscenium arch was dropping to bits, the loos were appalling, the seats in the circle and upper balcony were in many cases in shreds, and, worse, still, there were no seats whatsoever in the stalls as it had been used as a pop venue, where a thousand people would stand in the stalls area to listen to 'music', so loud that it was deafening and not really my scene.

However I had committed myself and I had to get on with it, with the added advantage that it constituted a real challenge. First we got together a group of trustees and had ourselves registered as a charity. The trustees represented accountancy, the media, one Member of Parliament, an actress/producer, the Head of the Liverpool Institute of Performing Arts which is really a 'university of the theatre' and grants degrees, and two or three more. They were always a pleasure to meet and to be with and tremendously co-operative although, of course, the most important person of all was Simon Geddes.

One thing I had insisted on was that we should have some good shows, and eventually – after about a year, we had a company putting on a good and serious play, 'The Sons of Ulster'. As we had no seats we had to bring in plastic chairs which were held together with tape. There was no heating – indeed not much of anything. A makeshift bar was set up, and off we went. To my great joy even in those conditions it was a success although I remember taking two grandchildren to another local theatre, the Everyman, near to Christmas time for the pantomime, and one of the comments from the stage was 'bloody freezing – like the Royal Court!"

The next play we had some months later was 'The Maids'. As Sonia and I walked from the car park to the Theatre it was pouring with rain and we were glad to get indoors. We sat down on our cold plastic chairs and the play started. The play was running, all seemed well, when suddenly large drops of water from the pouring rain outside started to drip on to the stage from the roof. I told Sonia that I was dashing out to ask Simon to put his thumb in the leaking hole in the roof, and keep it there until the show ended, when one of the 'maids' – it was a man as it happened – on another part of the stage, casually picked up his bucket, walked across to the dripping area, and happened to put the bucket down exactly where the drops were coming. That to me showed the true professional, and nobody in the audience ever remarked on the leaking roof because he caught it before it became a talking point.

We kept on applying for public money, from Northwest Arts, the Arts Council, the National Heritage, the Lottery, and Liverpool City Council, but all we got was £75,000 and that was our lot. The other theatres in Liverpool, the Everyman and the Playhouse, were receiving, so I was told, £1,000,000 per year from the City Council. The Empire – a commercial concern whilst we were a charitable trust – received, so I was informed, £7,000,000 from the City Council and from the National Lottery, and still we received nothing.

The then Heritage Secretary, Virginia Bottomly, came up to see the theatre and we stood on the stage together – there was no audience there! – and she promised to help. However before she could do this there was a General Election and the Conservative government fell. Although I visited the new government's National Lottery people in London and the Minister concerned we never received a penny. We never even got a formal lease from the City Council, who owned the building, and went on over the years virtually as 'tenants at will'.

Despite all these reverses we managed to move forward. Thelma Holt, of the Arts Council, managed to get the Royal Shakespeare Company to come up to put on the Merchant of Venice, which was excellent and very well received – but still no heating or seats. However at about that time we received our only grant – the £75,000 – and managed to get seats for the stalls. These were removable – they could be installed or removed in eight man-hours. That meant that the public could sit comfortably when the theatre was a theatre, and could be removed when there was a pop concert which was, of course, standing only. And gradually we managed, from ticket sales, to raise enough money to have carpeting as well. The reason for the pop concerts was that these were our only real source of income. There is little or no profit from 'culture' in the old sense. We even managed to install satisfactory heating.

One evening Sonia and I had taken two of the grandchildren, Alastair and Alexandra, to the Playhouse to see 'The Marriage of Figaro'. It was very well done, and then as we came out they asked if they could go to 'your theatre, Gramps', to a pop concert. We had never been to one but we agreed, as grandparents do when the grandchildren ask for anything. After all a grandchild's wish is a grandparent's command. We managed to get in past the bouncers, although with a suit and collar and tie and Sonia in a dress we looked most out of place. Simon took us up to the Circle where there were not many people. But the noise, and I mean noise, was deafening. He managed to get some ear-plugs for us which helped a bit, but only a bit.

The seats in the stalls had been removed for the occasion, and in the stalls area there must have been well over a thousand people, with the band playing from the stage amplified to full volume. Then they started 'surfing' which we had never seen before: Somebody from the back was passed by hand over the heads of all the people in front of him or her, up to the orchestra pit, and then put down, presumably in order to be recycled. And people had actually paid to have that done to them!

Gradually, gradually, with what money we could get from ticket and bar sales, we reinstated the Theatre. The Queen Mary Bar – modelled on the original ship of the same name – was restored to it original style and decoration, the old carpets removed and the original black and white floor revealed, The proscenium arch was repaired, the walls were restored, the loos were made respectable, the chandeliers were lowered and cleaned, and by about 2002 the Theatre was restored to its pristine glory.

We had a grand re-opening concert. The theatre was packed. After the interval I went on the stage to say my few words. I had not been on a big theatre stage before and it was an interesting experience. I had a concealed microphone with a transmitter attached to my bottom – with trousers in between – and what I said seemed to go down well. I knew the Theatre so well that talking about it was no problem, and there had been enough amusing incidents over the years to cover the comedy part. The problem was, and I had never experienced this before, that whilst the audience could hear everything I said, I could not see them because the floodlights were on me, and whilst there were microphones from the stage to the audience, that did not operate vice versa and so whilst sound carries wonderfully well from the stage to the auditorium I found that it did not work the other way round. So there was I speaking and hoping that I was getting the right reactions. I could vaguely hear laughter from time to time, and some applause indeed, but I could still not be sure that things had gone well. It was only afterwards that my mind was set at rest, and I was told that there was indeed genuine laughter and applause.

Then, as arranged, six-foot plus Simon came to join me, in front of the main curtain of course. I took one look up at him - and he is so much taller than me - and then, also of course by arrangement, a small stepladder was passed through the gap in curtains on to the stage. I climbed up until Simon and I were on the level and face to face and then after a short conversation and Simon's few words the show continued. The audience loved it,

We carried on like this until 2005 but we still had no formal lease and still no money, and Simon, who had devoted years to it for no great income, asked, and we agreed, that he should hand over the Theatre to somebody else. Eventually it went to a theatre club, Rawhide, and we can only hope that it prospers. At least we had done all we could and at least it was still being used as a theatre, and could be reconverted – although at this time it remains to be seen whether or not it will be – on a temporary or permanent basis to a straight theatre.

Anyway being retired we should have had a lot of time. A friend once said to me that when you retire you will still have a full diary for the forthcoming days and weeks, but as they are your own appointments and not those of clients or patients, you will not have to do them if you do not wish to. That seemed to me to be very sensible. However I found that he was wrong – because, as they are your own appointments and not somebody else's, and you made them because you wanted to, your diary remained as full as it had ever been.

One thing we could do more freely was to travel, not being limited by surgeries or the office, nor, indeed, by political commitments. One of the early major holidays was to South America, where we started in Chile – Santiago – then we went down to Bariloche and then up to Buenos Aires. I will not go through every place where we stopped, but when in Brazil we were able to see the Iguaçu Falls from above in a light aircraft and from a boat below, and these falls rank with, although I think that they are more impressive and greater than, the Victoria and Niagara Falls. But to see them from above and from below was a particular experience not to be forgotten.

We visited Argentina too, and whilst in Buenos Aires we found that the Liverpool Chamber of Commerce had arranged for us to meet the Chairman (a woman) of the Buenos Aires Chamber. She was a charming woman and asked us if we would like to join her the next day when the President of the Argentine, Carlos Menhem, was going to open a large new facility nor too far away. We immediately agreed, although it meant leaving the hotel at 6.30 in the morning, a time of day (or night?) I prefer not to recognize, and there was an enormous reception with all the Argentinean V.I.P.s – and us! The proceedings went well – they were in Spanish but it was the sort of function which would be the same the world over – and there were good eats and drinks. Then the Chamber of Commerce Chairman asked if we would like to meet the President personally. Of course we would! So we were duly introduced and had a chat in English, and then he had to leave – in his private helicopter. He was, at least to us, very friendly and easy to talk to and to listen to.

I busied myself more than previously, as I had more time for myself, to make videos of the various holidays and to make them into proper documentaries. It is interesting for me to recall that after years of cine filming, I had, a few years before, gone on to a video camera – which weighed about five kilos, which I carried on my shoulder. I could not record sound on it – it was not a camcorder, as they had not yet been invented - and so I had to wire it with a thirty foot cable to the videotape recorder under the television. One day my mother-in-law came in and I pointed the camera at her and, of course, there she was on the television screen and being recorded at the same time. She looked at the screen, then at me, then at the screen again, in absolute wonder, not knowing what had hit her. I still have this video, and what a treasure it is, to see the expression on the face of a lady where, when she was born, there was hardly a car to be seen, no cinemas certainly in Lithuania where she came from, and no 'mod cons', in any sense, at all. It was wonderful to see her amazement at this piece of the latest technology. The expression on her face said it all, save that she improved even on that by looking from camera to screen and back and, when looking at me, said in absolute wonder, 'It's me!'. I still have the tape of that and it is one of my treasures.

At this time Sonia continued to write articles for various journals, including the Jewish Telegraph, the Jewish Chronicle, and the Liverpool Daily Post – and there were others - on a variety of subjects, and I wrote a few as well. I was asked to be on the Liverpool University Law Faculty Committee which was raising money for the Law School.

Then in 1995 we decided to enlarge the house a little more. This was the third enlargement since the house was built and was to be the final one. We decided to extend the dining room, which, whilst adequate, had never been quite as we wanted it, and at the same time we improved the porch and vestibule. The exercise went extremely well, improving not only our living conditions but also the exterior of the house.

Writing continued, Alastair had his Barmitzvah, and I had undertaken another commitment: I had been on the Council of the Liverpool Chamber of Commerce for many years, but was appointed to be, at this time, Chairman of their Police Liaison Committee, which was concentrating on improving policing in Merseyside with the natural and intended consequence of improving trade and industry – the objectives of the Chamber. At the same time we were both Deputies on the Board of Deputies of British Jews – like a Jewish parliament. And there came a very pleasant surprise - I received a legacy of £125 from a former grateful client! It was good to think that I had done things to the satisfaction of at least one client.

We visited Nadine and her family in Jerusalem as often as we reasonably could, and joined the International Association of Jewish Lawyers and Jurists. They held in 1996 a very interesting conference in Tel Aviv, with lawyers attending from all over the world and in later years there were conferences elsewhere including Strasburg. It was with them that we visited Jordan, Amman the capital, Jerash, the Roman city with wonderful remains and, best of all, Petra, the sixth century B.C.E. Nabatean city, which had been on the main trade route, and its state of repair was remarkable. The buildings are world-renowned, and deserve to be. It is interesting to consider what they could do then, without modern machinery, power tools, or modern engineering. I wonder how many buildings built today will still be there in two thousand years' time. As we left Petra we were able, and could never resist the challenge, to return to base on horseback rather than in carriages, and this we did. We could still ride!

We continued to be members of the British Association of Jewish Studies, and in 1996 Sonia was asked to give a paper – I think the only non-academic ever to be asked. The subject was 'Snake Images in the Five books of Moses', and it went a bomb. She spent a lot of time on fascinating research and by the time you heard it you knew a lot more not only about snakes but also about Moses. I was particularly impressed – indeed so were they all – at this remarkable talk about how snakes were gradually eased out of Jewish culture – they could not be taken out in too much of a hurry. The BAJS is about 70/30 Jews and non-Jews. She received wonderful plaudits from the senior academics there. The Conference that year was made particularly exciting as it was at Cambridge – it is always held at the university where the president for the year has his patch. We stayed in a guest room – or rather I should say a suite – in St John's College. Of course 'John's' was founded by Henry VI and so is very wealthy and could afford to have that sort of accommodation. My College, Pembroke, was not, and is not, in the same wealthy league, although apparently it is the third most popular college in the University, and the guest rooms there are adequate but far from palatial. Sonia gave several more papers at these Conferences. She was not only complimented but told by several senior professors that she was the best speaker at the conference – as indeed she was. She presented a lecture, and did not just, as did so many, 'read a paper'.

More cruises followed, including the Baltic capitals and St. Petersburg, with all it has to offer, and it has a lot to offer. The Winter Palace, where the Tsars lived in such splendour, were fortunately left intact by the Communist regime and has now been brought up again to the standard which must have applied in Tsarist days. The design, art galleries, furnishings, everything were such that we were reluctant to leave and may still, one day, return. Contrasting with this beautiful complex were appalling tall blocks where apparently toilets were shared between two or more flats, and the road surfaces were dangerously poor for vehicles and for pedestrians. Then on this Baltic cruise we visited the capital of every country we passed.

At home we were both asked to speak to various organizations about all sorts of things – and still are - and there was an occasional appearance on television as well. One of the best parts of our retirement, though, and it still continues to give me great pleasure, is that (and forgive me if I am being repetitive) whenever we walk round the Crosby area Sonia is still stopped by former patients telling her how much they miss her.

From about this time, having settled down in our retirement, we decided to do some long-haul holidays to see places we had never seen before and were not likely to see again. But we have never, and never shall, visit Germany, and even the language is so painful to our ears after the atrocities of the War. So many members of our families had died in German hands, and one still may meet some of those responsible, or their children who could have been infected. Indeed we did stop in Germany once, through the Israel Air Line, El Al! It was supposed to be a direct flight from Manchester to Tel Aviv, and then made an unscheduled stop at Frankfurt, I think to pick up some freight. The passengers were allowed off to sit in the departure lounge for the hour or so but we chose to remain in the aircraft while they cleaned it, but even the very sound of the voices of the Germans working outside was enough to upset us.

We decided, after a lot of debate, to visit Japan. They had been as wicked in as many, although somewhat different, ways as the Germans, but they did not select just Jews to be taken to the slaughter, but everybody whom they saw fit to dispose of. We were uncomfortable there but at least we felt it possible to go there. We visited the usual temples and tourist sights, and saw as much of the non-tourist parts as we could. It took some time getting used to the custom that if you met anybody you did not shake hands but gave a slight bow. The system was, so I understood, that the junior one bowed more deeply, and first, and the senior one replied with a more gentle bow. We always treated ourselves as being of the upper echelon.

The cleanliness was impressive, but one amazing thing was the discipline of the people: If there was a light-controlled pedestrian crossing the people waiting to cross – stopped by the red light – and did not move even if there was no sign of traffic in sight. Then when they changed to green, across they ran or walked. Eating was alright if one was careful not to eat what we westerners consider to be outrageous food – snake, for example - but even with the shorter Japanese chopsticks it was more than satisfactory. The hotels were magnificent.

We visited one fantastic Shinto temple there. As we walked round the gardens and parks there was a very large lake, round which most people walked. However there was a stepping-stone ford across the middle, and there was I with my camcorder seeing an opportunity to take some unusual views from the middle of the lake. I stepped out, and then again and again moved from stone to stone, stopping to take pictures. Then I stepped off again, thinking that the stones were equidistant, but

I had come to a stone which was not as equidistant as the others, and they were a little wet as well. I misjudged and I went into the water up to my neck. The most important thing was not me but the camcorder, so I held it high like Excalibur and it, and only it, remained dry.

I managed to get out, my video saved, and I was absolutely soaking. However it was a warm day so the cold water was no problem. I said to Sonia that we should return to the bus with the others on the tour. She thought – quite rightly as usual – that I was mad, but I insisted. When we got to the bus not surprisingly they would not let me in, so there was no alternative but to take a taxi back to the hotel. The taxis in Tokyo are quite smart cars with chauffeurs wearing white gloves, and with white seat covers to see that the passengers were kept spotless. This caused a problem to the taxi driver who saw this soaking muddy figure wishing to enter his spotlessly clean vehicle. However he allowed us in and back to the hotel we went. The camcorder was carefully placed on the dressing table to dry out any dampness which may have got into it, and I stripped down for a bath. The water when I got out was nearly black. Then Sonia put in fresh water and put my clothes in for a bath. It was amazing how much mud and dirt came off them – and I had intended to continue the tour in that condition!

We took the bullet train to travel west. It was a stopping train. When we got to the platform to await the train's arrival the taxi driver who had taken us to the station told us where to stand and told us that that was where our seats would be. I asked him to stand by in case the train was a yard or two out of line, so that he could help us with the cases, but he told me not to worry. He was right. The train drew up exactly – and I mean exactly – where we stood, and in we went. The carriage was rather like the business class cabin in an aircraft. Further along were the first class carriages, in a double-deck part of the train. The 'seats' were in fact individual rooms, equipped with armchairs and settees and, so far as I recall, computers and probably televisions. The dining car was like a good restaurant.

I went to the loo: There was the usual Far Eastern type of loo which was a hole in the floor, but it was spotlessly clean. There was another loo next door which was the European type and I preferred that. I did what I had to do and when I was about to stand up I noticed some buttons on the right of me next to the seat, with Japanese writing on them. I nearly pressed one but I feared that it might be an ejector seat, so I concluded what I had to do in the usual way. I learned subsequently that had I pressed the button it would have done for me all that I had had to do for myself, and probably even better! Even in the washbasin the taps poured water on to your hands when it knew they were there – there was no need to turn a tap. That is more common these days but at that time it was quite extraordinary. It shows how quickly things change.

It was a stopping train, and so only reached about 250 miles an hour. It stopped and started within seconds of due time, and when we arrived the person meeting us was standing in the right place as he knew precisely where the train would stop. The other remarkable thing about the journey was its quietness, one hardly felt the acceleration and the deceleration, and were it not for signs giving us the speed we would never have believed it. It was just a far far better ride than, over ten years later, Virgin trains could manage from Liverpool to London!

From there we flew to Korea. The hotel in Seoul was again magnificent and all mod cons and more. Korea had been occupied by the Japanese for very many decades and, not unnaturally, the Koreans did not like their former occupiers. One of the most interesting but disturbing visits was to the northern frontier, with North Korea on the other side. The frontier was not of the friendly type we had met hitherto, but a real frontier, militarily manned and with no contact with the north. One could look across from a watch-tower but that was all, and there was nothing, and no movement, to be seen.

They told us about, and we saw, tunnels which some years before had been dug by the North Koreans under the frontier from North to South to enable several battalions of North Korean troops to enter the south unobserved, and then mount a full invasion. They had to dig the tunnel with the help of high explosives, and had had a dummy 'factory' on their side of the border which required occasional explosions in the course of producing whatever they were supposed to be producing. We were told

- 163 -

that the explosions in the factory were timed precisely to coincide with the explosions which were part of the tunnel excavations, so they were not observed. The Americans in due course, after investigation, found the tunnels and sealed them off before the invasion could take place. We were taken through one of the tunnels. They could easily have housed more than a London Underground train, with many details to facilitate the easy movement of troops. It was quite terrifying. Out at sea, too, were patrolling destroyers and other naval ships, not crossing the hidden border but at all times on the alert.

Another place which will indelibly be left in our memories was Pusan in the south. That was the corner to which the Allies were driven by the North Koreans until General McArthur, the American in command, carried out a landing at Seoul and carried out a pincer movement from there and eventually defeated the invaders. It was an interesting drive down to Pusan, with many temples and towns. In one temple there was an enormous bell, probably nearly twenty feet high, which could be rung by having a horizontal wooden pole suspended alongside it, and the monks would pull back the pole a foot or two, and the let go so that it hit the bell and a loud clear tone came forth.

The legend was that the monks required such a bell, and made one. But the sound was not clear. And so the religious leader said that the only way to do it was to put a young girl in the molten metal and then use the boiled or molten remains of the girl to make the bell give a clear sound. The tale runs that a young girl of about eight years was taken from her widowed mother, screaming, and put in the molten metal. The bell was then made and the sound was perfect, reflecting the clear cries of the child.

That was on the way south, and then we arrived in Pusan. During the Korean War there had been a tremendous number of British troops involved. To go back quite a few years I remembered that at the start of the Korean War they called up, in this country, troops who had been demobilized from World War II, and they were known as the 'Z' reserve. To my horror I found that I was one of them, and I suppose as a trained infantry officer could have been quite useful. By that time we were married and Sonia was pregnant. Having served in the army for four years I was reluctant to be involved again, particularly with a potential offspring on the way. However I was summoned for a medical. On the day I was due to go I was engaged in court, and so I telephoned to change the date, which was agreed.

The first appointment had been, I was told, a day for former officers, but the day I actually went was an 'other ranks' day. This being so, and class distinction being what it was in those days, I was dealt with first. I went through with no problems, as fit as a fiddle. The final doctor asked me if there was anything wrong with me at all. I replied that I was one hundred per cent fit – and this took a bit of quick thinking – but that my flat feet still troubled me. I had in fact suffered from flat feet since childhood and had had quite a bit of pain, but whilst in the army and marching for many miles, I am pleased to say that I never had a moment of trouble. The doctor asked me what the problems were, and I took my memory back some years and recalled the sort of pain from which I had suffered. But, I told him, it was something I would have to deal with – stiff upper lip and all that. He pressed me and eventually I 'reluctantly' admitted that I still suffered if I walked any distance at all. I then left and awaited my call-up papers. Instead I received a letter to tell me that I was medically unfit for service in Korea and would not be called up. What a relief! But Sonia nevertheless gave me the most thorough medical examination I had ever had to make sure there really was nothing wrong.

So to get back to Korea, where I visited fortunately as a civilian and not as an army officer, we, out of respect, visited the military cemetery. We make a point of visiting war cemeteries, wherever we are. It was all British. It was a dull and rainy day, but we visited as many graves we could in the hour or two we spent there. In the time we were there we counted four Victoria Crosses. I was then, and still am, very moved at the thought. We went to sign the visitors' book. They had difficulty in finding it because there were so few visitors. The parents of those who were killed were long dead or too old to travel so far, and the wives would have remarried and made new lives. The sadness of those memories will forever remain with us.

-oOo-

Chapter 16
Doing Our Own Thing

B ut 1997 was not just a year when we went on such a fascinating holiday, but was also a year for celebrating events. We celebrated my birthday, Sonia's birthday and, almost as important, the 650th birthday of my College, Pembroke at Cambridge. Founded in 1347 and with some of the original 14th Century buildings still there, I still feel very close to Pembroke and treat her as one of the family. We try to make an annual visit for a week-end, and the annual Garden Party, just to keep an eye on it. Also during 1997 a new Court (or courtyard, or range of buildings) was being completed known as Foundress Court, after the Foundress, Marie de St Pol de Valence, Countess of Pembroke. It is a very modern building, I like it very much, it is very comfortable and incorporates the Master's Lodge, where the Master of the College lives. I thoroughly enjoy walking through a 14th Century gateway, through a court – or courtyard – in which stands Sir Christopher Wren's first work, the College Chapel, through to the Elizabethan Court and on the New Court, built in the 19th Century. Now we come to a 20th Century addition. Another college which does this very well is St John's College, quite new by Pembroke standards – built in the time of King Henry VI – but there again one sees the signs of time and centuries in the buildings. Some people criticised the post-war concrete blocks at the other side of the river as being out of context, but how dull it would be if they continued to build in exactly the same style as the original buildings.

Foundress Court was not completed until fairly late in 1997 and so it was not a practicable proposition to have a celebration that year. In the circumstances it was arranged that the May Ball – which as its name implies, always takes place in June – should be planned for 1998. The last May Ball I had attended was in 1947 when, back from Africa and the War being over, I, still being in the army, hired a set of Blue Patrols – dark blue dress uniform with all the braiding and spurs – and was able to get leave to attend. A May Ball goes on all night from 10pm until six in the morning when the "Survivors' Photograph" is taken and it is much more than just a dance. There is entertainment of all kinds including food and shows and it is a wonderful time for reminiscences, and so this May Ball in 1998 was to follow the same pattern.

Sonia and I stayed at the University Arms Hotel and then dressed up and went to the Ball to be there right at the start – about 10pm. It was a 'white tie and tails' affair although unfortunately white tie and tails are fading out (and I have not had the opportunity to wear it since), except for May Balls and very special occasions of a similar nature. It was a wonderful opportunity to wear my C.B.E. round my neck and look important. It was a rainy night, which was unfortunate, but that did not dampen the spirit of the celebration. There were marquees for eating and dancing, and every part of the College was used for some different entertainment. So one could dance, eat, watch performances, eat again in a different place and style, listen to music of varied kinds – and I had no trouble keeping awake. My brother Eric and his wife Inge left at 2am but we were determined to see it through, and in due course at 6 o'clock on the following morning we were all assembled in Ivy Court and photographed as the 'Survivors'.

The most important happening in 1999 was the fact that by then we had been married for fifty years and a Golden Wedding is really something: That is particularly so when, after that period of time, we still felt towards each other even more than we had done fifty years before. Until this day when we have our 'good-morning kiss' it is no formality but we hug each other and mean it. And so the Anniversary was quite a thing. We were in Jerusalem at the time and had we been left to our own devices we would probably have gone away for the weekend, had dinner together and danced and had the joy of each other's company. But Nadine was not prepared to leave it at that. She had arranged a special party for us at the Hartman Institute in Jerusalem and had invited the people she knew we would prefer to be with at a party, but we knew nothing of the details until we arrived.

She had montages of photographs of many things which had happened during our fifty years, including newspaper cuttings and anything else of interest, excellent food, and she and her family put on a wonderful show with musical accompaniment of how Sonia and I met. Nadine had asked to borrow the jacket Sonia wore the first time I set eyes on her, which we had kept sentimentally, and they had also borrowed my army slouch hat from my days in Africa, and between them and the children they re-enacted our meeting with great accuracy and with musical accompaniment. Inbal played the part of Sonia and Elad played me, and it was most professionally done, and all the words and songs – although not the music – were original. Then we were asked, without proper warning – and we knew nothing of anything until it happened and so the element of surprise was there the whole time – to give a little speech. I did mine and then Sonia did hers – in Hebrew. She did it so well that one friend of ours who speaks a good English said that having heard Sonia speak in Hebrew he would never speak to her in English again.

It was in 1998 as well that the International Institute of Jewish Lawyers and Jurists decided to hold its big annual event that year in Strasburg. We had been to conferences in Israel and London, the one in New York had been too far to go for a conference, but Strasburg was within reach and there we flew. We knew a lot of the people there from previous conferences and to be with lawyers from the world over was and is always interesting. But this conference was in many ways different from the others we had attended. One was that it was in France, and the head of the French delegation managed to displease quite a number of people as he was to a certain extent in charge. I was one of those critics. One thing which annoyed us particularly was that he, and it appeared to be the local custom, had no sense of timing. One evening some presentations were to be made at about six o'clock, and with only about three of them dinner by eight o'clock would seem to have been no problem. What we had not taken into consideration, though, was that each speech of thanks would last for about half an hour, and as they were usually about people we did not know they were not the most interesting talks in the world. The response is normally 'thank you' and an acceptance of some gift. But not here, oh no! The 'thank you' was another half hour, and there were three presentations altogether.

We must add to this the introductory speeches and the concluding speeches with the result that we eventually got down to dinner for about 10pm, to find that they had a peculiar arrangement of tables, so that some were serving kosher food, some vegetarian, and some non-kosher, all poorly signed and with very little help from the organizers and the service was appalling. So far as I recall we left a part-eaten meal at about ten thirty and went to bed. There were other instances of this as well, including a very interesting series of talks on the Friday afternoon which were due to finish at four o'clock. We left at about five-thirty and they were still going strong.

However there were compensations, and one was to see the buildings and settings of the European Parliament in Strasburg. We had appreciated that the Parliament shuttled between Brussels and Strasburg, but had not realised the extent or cost of the shuttle. Apparently the Parliament sat, and still sits, in Brussels for three weeks each month, and then moves to Strasburg for the other week. That means that not only hundreds – literally – of Members of the European Parliament move over, but also all the civil servants and, worse still, the paper, move over too. The buildings and accommodation were superb – naturally, because we and not they were paying for it – but it is difficult even now, years later, and it is continuing, to comprehend such vast expense and inconvenience to no purpose other than to satisfy the French desire to have the European Parliament in their country too. I wonder what would happen if every country felt and acted the same way – the whole parliament, civil servants, and paper would have to move from one country to another every day! Indeed when we flew to Strasburg from Manchester we had to change 'planes in Brussels on the way out and Paris on the way back. There are no direct flights. The aircraft in each case were Boeing 737s, and the whole of the front half of the aircraft was Business Class, and the rest was for the likes of us. The only difference between Business class and the commoners was a few inches of legroom, but the cost differential was considerable. The front half – the expensive half – was almost empty. The reason was that it was only full when the Parliament was moving, when all concerned travelled in the Business Class area at no expense to them – only to us as the European taxpayers. We had never been particularly pro-European up till then, and that experience did not help. In fact I think that even when the Members of the European Parliament travel, many of them travel Economy Class but get paid for Business Class – but this, of course, could be idle gossip. The good part, though, was that the people attending, and the lectures, were of the same high standard as always at these conferences, the lectures being in English or French. In the latter those who required it could get an immediate translation with earphones.

- 170 -

We continued with our foreign travels, usually travelling on Swan Hellenic's Minerva – 'the culture boat' as we always call it – but we went on a Renaissance Cruise round the Mediterranean. I mention these not because I wish to bore you with a detail of each port of call – although they were all good – but to mention that on each such cruise I make a video. The taking of the video sometimes makes me a little unpopular from time to time, I suppose, but if we are with a guided group I ask the guide to give me some information as to what he or she is about to say to the group in a minute's time. The guide invariably says that I shall hear it all in a moment, but when I explain why I want it beforehand they normally help and tell me. Then whilst the group listens to the guide I do my filming and speak my commentary into a special microphone so that it is clear when played back. That way the commentary is spontaneous, bang up-to-date, and makes all the difference not only to what I say but how I say it. If, for example, I have climbed to the top of a South American pyramid and I am a bit – or a lot! – puffed, this comes out in the commentary and gives the audience an indication of the realities, rather than being a stuffy talk from the comfort of an armchair. After each filming session I usually find that the group has moved on, so I have to tear off, get ahead of them, approach the guide again for the next lot of information, and then repeat my performance.

When I get back home I probably have about four hours of tape which I must then edit down to not more than an hour. The reason for this is that a lot of people do not have the time or patience to watch for more than an hour. I would rather they saw 'The End' whilst wanting more, rather than that they should be relieved that the film is over.

With modern computing programmes I can edit to an accuracy of $1/25^{th}$ second, and add transitions, titles, music, sound effects, picture-in-picture, and all the professional niceties. Were I to rewrite this paragraph in five years' time, if I am still alive and kicking, what I have just written will be old hat. Technology will have improved even more. Of course each holiday or cruise is not just a couple of weeks, but probably another month on my return to edit it, and then another week or two to make copies for various friends to whom I have promised them.

It was about this time we changed one of the cars – the Senator – for a Lexus 200, the latest Japanese car which had, and indeed continues to have, most favourable reports in every respect and was indeed called the 'Japanese Rolls Royce'. Well, we did not have the largest top model which may well have compared with the Rolls, but a smaller one well big enough for the two of us and any family or friends we chose to take with. The interesting thing about it was that it was fitted with what was, then, the very latest technology, which consisted not only of 'climate control' as opposed to air conditioning, which had previously been the latest thing, or cruise control which had been there before, but a GPS – satellite navigation. This is so common now but then it was something that our friends would come round to see as a tremendous novelty. It has saved us literally hundreds of hours which would otherwise have been spent in getting lost. In fact in 2009 the most expensive Lexus is able to back into a parking space by itself and with no interference by the driver, without hitting anything. If you are sleepy it will blow cold air into your face to keep you awake. Further, if you are on Cruise Control and getting too near to the car in front, you will automatically slow down.

Early that year we went to Israel for another break, and this time went to the Golan Heights. It was quite extraordinary to be on a sledge, or in a cable car over the snow, or seeing the skiers, in Israel which people regard as always being at least warm and usually hot. But in May of that year we went from cold to heat and visited classical Campania in Italy. We went with a group called Andante Travel, a small group of about twelve, with a lecturer and 'nanny', and were kept thoroughly busy for a week not only seeing, but having explained to us, what we saw. We visited, near Naples, the Temple of Athena in a fantastic state of preservation and the murals, some 2000 years old, were quite unbelievable. But the most moving and impressive of all was Pompeii, where you can see the stone moulds, which had formed themselves round the corpses of those killed in the eruption, and which remain to this day. We visited an amphitheatre where you could see exactly where the gladiators had eaten, slept, and lived and died, and walking up Vesuvius we were not allowed to go too high because it was erupting in a mild way, and smoke, steam and occasional flames were in our way. If you picked up a stone it was warm – or sometimes hot.

Another interesting holiday that year, just for a week, was Prague. Many of you will know it and it is a delightful and fascinating city – we found that there were about thirty, or more, concerts available every evening. We went to one playing Mozart with the players in the dress and using the instruments of the time, in a disused church: Indeed most of the concert halls were disused churches. We met a group of young Englishmen and their girl friends dressed up as batman or similar characters, inebriated but very pleasant, and asked them what they were doing there. They explained that one of them was getting married the following week and this was to celebrate the forthcoming event. The great advantage of Prague was, we were told, that the beer was cheap, cheap enough indeed to outweigh the cost of getting there. We asked where was the bride-to-be but were told that she was at home looking after the baby.

One morning before we went out we were in our hotel room. Sonia asked me to pass her handbag. It needed a two-ton winch to lift it and I asked politely what the hell was in it. We emptied it out and only put back the hankies and lipstick, leaving her with a handbag instead of a cabin trunk. Then we went out and decided to try out the Metro, their fairly new underground train service. It was most impressive and we went to catch a train, just for one stop, on the way to the town centre. I took my usual video and when I watched it later I could see that the approaching train was fairly empty. However as we were getting in there was quite a crowd, and we were stuck near the doors, one of us at one side and one at the other, with masses of people milling and we could only just see each other. As the train started to move a chap next to me suggested that I should hold the overhead rail in case I fell, but I was so crammed in nothing could have knocked me over. I was a little suspicious, but was confident as my wallet was very well concealed.

When we came to the first station its doors only opened with difficulty with the pressure of people against them, but we managed to get out. As we did an American called out to warn us to check our pockets as he felt that some people had been mugged. We duly checked. I was fine with my concealed wallet and with nothing in my pockets except a handkerchief. I realised then why I had been asked to hold the overhead rail – so that my jacket pockets would have been more accessible.

So far as Sonia was concerned every zip on her handbag, and there were four or five, was unzipped, but as we had emptied it in the hotel nothing was taken as there was nothing to take. But her watch, bracelet, and a necklace were missing. With the crush she had not felt a thing. When we got back to England we claimed from the insurance company and they duly and promptly paid up. The necklace was of gold, bought in Singapore, done like a snake and we were very sorry to lose it, but at least we recovered from the insurers the £700 which was the replacement cost – although it would have been very difficult to find a replacement for such an unusual necklace. Some three months later Sonia was looking through her little 'jewellery' roll and – there it was! – the necklace! We both thought that she had been wearing it but it must have been in the hotel all the time, in the safe in our room. So I immediately wrote to the insurers explaining the position, apologising for the claim, and enclosing a cheque for £700 by way of reimbursement. I received a reply quite soon afterwards which read:- "We acknowledge receipt of your letter and cheque. Yours faithfully.!" My own view is that it was more trouble to them to reopen the file to put the £700 back than that if we had kept the money. The strange thing is that if the same thing happened again I would do the same again because you have to live with yourself.

During 2001 we had a delightful cruise, again on Minerva, round Italy and Sicily, including among others such wonderful places as Ravenna, Venice, Bari, Naples, Ostia and Lucca. However during this cruise I had, from time to time, some pain in my right hip. Sonia had her views but nevertheless she advised that we took a second opinion from the ship's doctor. He asked me to walk round his surgery, had a chat, never even put me on the couch, and said that I had probably strained a muscle. Sonia still had her doubts and from time to time I still had my pain.

-oOo-

Chapter 17
Under The Knife

On our return to Liverpool we went to see an orthopaedic surgeon, Stephen Montgomery, to see what he thought. He said that it appeared to be arthritic deterioration in my right hip and sent me further up Rodney Street – the Harley Street of Liverpool, every address being either doctors or dentists or related professions – to have an X-Ray. This was a private visit, but nevertheless the X-Ray machine really came out of the Ark. One had to climb high on to it – I was glad to be able to do that – and then when the machinery started to work one got the impression of being in a factory with all the machinery running. If my hip had been alright before that I am sure that the climbing up and down did it no good.

Going for the X-Ray, and the walk up Rodney Street was only about two hundred yards, my hip was not too bad, but going back to see Steve Montgomery it was suddenly extremely painful and we had to pause a time or two before I could carry on. I wondered if climbing on to the ancient X-Ray machine was responsible. We gave the X-Ray to Steve and, showing it to us, he explained that there was arthritic deterioration, but that it was not too bad and I should be able to carry on for quite some time. I told him again that the pain really had been unpleasant, and he arranged that I should be scheduled for a hip replacement on 19th December but he advised that I could cancel it at any time, even the same day, if I had no need for it. He really never expected any rapid deterioration and I was very encouraged. When Sonia had advised further investigation and not to rely on the ship's doctor, she was absolutely right.

However the pain got worse and worse, and some days I could not even cross the kitchen at home, and if I had one day's remission, I would have the pain returning the next day. So we decided that we should go ahead. On 19th December I went - Sonia was with me of course – to the Sefton Suite, the private hospital wing of Aintree University Hospital. One thing I do not like about private hospitals is that generally they do not have an intensive care unit should it be necessary, nor supplies of blood or spare parts. But the Sefton Suite, built within the main hospital, has everything on the spot, and even the operating theatre is within the hospital, although exclusively for the use of the Sefton Suite, and is one hundred per cent up to date.

The Sefton Suite is very comfortable, and they were able to arrange for Sonia to have a room across the corridor so that she could come to see me any time of day or night. So that afternoon I went for a final X-Ray and when they came back with the plate and showed it to Steve Montgomery he was quite surprised at the deterioration. It really was bad and the operation not only went ahead, but very much needed to.

I was taken in the trolley to the theatre and Sonia accompanied me to the door, giving me a 'good luck' kiss before I was wheeled in. Once in the ante-room I had to have the spinal anaesthetic. The anaesthetist asked me if I wanted to be awake and hear what went on, although I would feel no pain. I elected, coward that I am, that I would prefer to feel no pain and to hear no operation, so out I went. Whilst 'out' I dreamt that I heard a circular saw, like cutting wood. A few days later I told this to the anaesthetist, explaining to her that obviously I was dreaming. She said that I was not dreaming at all, I had indeed heard a circular saw, but it was cutting my bone and not a piece of wood.

I was taken back to my room, with Sonia waiting for me, and did not feel too bad, as the anaesthetic had not worn off. Indeed I was quite bright in the circumstances. After an hour or so, though, the anaesthetic wore off and, as was to be anticipated, the pain started to come where Steve had operated. Then Sonia noticed that I had passed out. How fortunate it was that she was with me, as indeed it always is. I was immediately given a blood transfusion, and I had pipes all over me for things to come in and things to go out, and this brought me round. Eventually I went to sleep with the help of the appropriate drugs. However during the night I felt very uncomfortable particularly as after a hip operation one has to lie on one's back with one's legs apart and with a cushion in between, which to me is a most unsatisfactory position. So I called the nurse and she took me across, with the help of a zimmer, to an armchair. Whilst sitting there I looked up and there was Sonia, who must have been listening and popping in to ensure that I was alright, coming to see how I was getting on. She really was, as she always has been, absolutely wonderful and the very sight of her made me feel better. We chatted for a while and then I was put back to bed with more drugs and got to sleep.

The next day I was up using a zimmer. The day after that I was on two crutches. The day after that I was on two walking sticks, and the day after it was one. The next day I climbed a few stairs – under the careful supervision of the physiotherapists - and on the sixth day we went home. Whilst we were in hospital Steve, who was not only very competent but a very caring person, came to visit me every day. He told me that after he had replaced the hip he measured up and found that one leg was about a centimetre longer than the other. So he removed the new hip and put in its place one of the right size, and my legs have been thereafter precisely the same length.

It was painful but I could cope, and each day there was an improvement – the only real problem being, as I have said, sleeping on my back with a pillow between my legs, and that had to go on for six weeks. To stop me turning over by mistake each evening Sonia put a barrier up between me and what had been her side of the bed, and whilst she slept in another room she came in several times each night to see how I was getting on. We went for longer and longer walks, and this experience will be common to any reader who has undergone the same thing. At the end of six weeks I was beginning to feel reasonably alright and was sleeping reasonably well. I wanted to be well enough to get to our grandson's, Asaf's, barmitzvah in Jerusalem on 16th March, and that was our aim. We managed to do it and flew out a few days before, which was only just 12 weeks or so after the operation. Steven Montgomery had done a good job.

The barmitzvah went excellently and I took video of it to edit it into a proper 'film' afterwards. At one stage Sonia noticed that I was standing on a chair to get a better shot of the proceedings, and gently but very firmly got me down to ground level, telling me, quite rightly, that I was mad, and making me promise not to do it again. Without Sonia's care and help I could never have got on so quickly or so well, nor would I have got to the barmitzvah.

Chapter 18
Back To 'Retirement'

The following year we decided to try something a bit different – a 'bus cruise' round New England and French Canada. We landed in New York, went to the designated hotel, and then we all – not too many of us – got on to a very good quality coach for our tour. This was run by a firm called Tauk, and they were as good as their word, save that 'cruising' on land instead of by sea meant packing and unpacking every day or, at best, every other day. Also sitting in a coach, however comfortable, is not like the freedom of wandering about a boat, with libraries, films, good dining and all the other things which go with it,

We went to Boston where some of Sonia's relatives live – and unlike many relatives, they are nice people. In addition Boston is a lovely city which boasts, as well, the oldest University in the United States, Harvard, which is particularly attractive as Harvard, the founder, was a Cambridge man. From there we went to the rocky coast of Maine, and on the beach we saw 'sand sculptures' the like of which we have not see before or since. There were people, buildings – even a Statue of Liberty – all made of sand and perfectly sculptured. There were many of them, large, and each as remarkable as the others. The weather, it appeared, was calm enough not to blow them away or wreck them with rain.

Then we entered into French Canada, and these days it really is French. At the border we changed from miles to kilometres, all the signs were in French – even 'danger' signs were not translated. When dealing with the local population it might have been alright if they had spoken French French, but it was, of course, Quebecois, the French Canadian version. They could understand us but we found it extremely difficult to understand them. I know that it was more recent than Chaucer's English, but it is still old enough for the language to have changed a great deal. The writing was clear enough but speech was impossible for us.

It was while we were in Montreal that we passed the 'Palais de Justice' – the Law Courts – and so we popped in to see if there was anything on. It was after lunch on Friday and all that was left was a murder trial, so up we went. The judge looked like an English judge but whilst he had no wig his robes were not far different from those of the English judiciary. He was finishing summing up to a jury – in English – and there was a frosted glass screen between the jury and the public gallery, where we were – so that the jurors could not be seen and so would not be 'nobbled' afterwards. A very good idea.

When the judge had finished and retired I went to the Clerk of the Court and explained that I had spent some time as a judge in England and that I would like to meet 'His Honour' to compare notes. I was wearing light blue trousers, a yellow shirt, my hair was untidy and I was laden with a camcorder and other travel equipment. She asked me for some identification, and all I could offer was my face. However she enquired of the judge and he invited us in to his chambers.

He was a Scotsman by birth and was the senior judge of Quebec Province. He was a delightful man and, of course, we spoke in English – but whenever one of the clerks came in for instructions the conversations were in Quebecois, in which the judge was fluent. I asked him why the trial we had seen was being conducted in English, and he explained that in a criminal case the language is the one requested by the defendant – which meant, of course, that not only the judge but the clerks and lawyers had to be completely bilingual. The system of law in the criminal courts, he told us, was English Law.

I asked him what happened in civil cases, and he said that the language used was that as agreed between the parties. In addition, as I had thought, the system of law was the Code Napoleon, French law, and so the judge, and those practising, had to be not only bilingual but they had to be completely conversant with two completely different systems of law. One result of this, we were told, was that American firms dealing commercially in Canada did not wish to have any controversial issues tried by a strange and foreign system of law. As a result a lot of commerce had moved from French Canada to Toronto, where the English system was so much more akin to that used in the United States.

It was in August of that year that our grandson Alastair was in Jerusalem during his 'gap year', and whilst there had arranged to meet a friend in the cafeteria of the Hebrew University. On his way there he was delayed by a lady who wanted to pick his brain about her computer. It was very inconvenient for him as it would make him late for his appointment but, true to his upbringing, he did as she asked and gave her the advice she required before carrying on towards the cafeteria. As he got to the corner there was a tremendous explosion – a suicide bomber had gone in and blown himself up with those eating there. Had Alastair been even a quarter of a minute earlier he would have been killed. His friend whom he had been going to meet was dead. The 'nuisance' woman had saved his life. He helped the ambulance people where he could, and as a good English speaker he was grabbed by pretty well all the television companies and, very fluently and lucidly, gave his views and comments in English on the spot. He was seen world-wide and we saw him here on the U.K. programmes. I think that it was the fact that these broadcasts kept him so busy for the hour or two after the bomb went off that he managed to ride the post-bomb trauma which one would normally have expected.

The following spring Sonia and I went for a week to Lithuania, where her parents were born and married. We flew into Vilnius International Airport. The luggage carousel was about the size of a large dining table and the airport would have made any of the provincial British airports look like Heathrow by comparison.

There was to be a car awaiting us, air-conditioned and automatic. There was a car, but the air-conditioning was not working and the automatic gearbox had broken down. The 'car man' took us in his car to Vilnius University where we could for a short time take part in a series of lectures, in a summertime course, in Yiddish, and he told us not to worry and that he would arrange another car for us. When we left the university to continue on our journey the car in which they had brought us was clamped! The police came and our guide or the man from whom we were renting the car carried the can and presumably paid any fines due. There was no argument and everything was very good-natured. So they got another car, an Alfa Romeo, and the gearbox worked – but the air-conditioning did not. So they then drove us away in yet another car – which had air conditioning - to Kaunas where we were staying the night, and after we had been there about an hour the car we had ordered not only arrived but worked. We were not aware at that time that there were very few, if any, new cars in Lithuania as nobody could afford them, and so they are virtually all second-hand.

Lithuania was a nostalgic stop in that we saw where Sonia's mother and father had probably lived, where they married and the synagogues where they worshipped – or what remained of those synagogues. Sonia's mum had told us that there was a visiting fair every year in Mariampole, and there it was. We saw people swimming in the Shishupe River of which she had spoken many times, and we probably were within a hundred yards or so of where she was born and lived. We sat in the train at the very station where they would have sat when they left Lithuania for the last time. My father-in-law had been in England for some time before that, having arrived there before the first World War. During the War he served in the 38th Royal Fusiliers in Palestine. He had then gone back to marry his first cousin, Sonia's mother, whom he had known from childhood. The story goes that when they were both in the British

Consulate arranging for my then future mother-in-law's name to be added to her future husband's passport. The Consul was most attentive and then excused himself for a few minutes whilst he arranged for the documents to be typed. Whilst he was out Sonia's Mum asked her Dad if the Consul was alive! "Why, of course! Why do you ask?' asked her father. The reply was that the whole time he had spoken to them he had not used his hands at all!

Our stay in Lithuania was very sad. The Lithuanians had been killing Jews even before Hitler arrived, we saw the ghettos and the killing fields – including one, the size of a large football pitch, where all the Jews of the small town of Mariampole, had been made to dig it out so that they could be shot by the Germans and thrown into it. All her relatives would have been there. Then there was the Ninth Fort in Kaunas where some 100,000 people, mostly Jews, had been murdered, and this was apart from the post-War K.G.B. headquarters where the Russians had managed to do their share of murdering and torturing, but here they 'dealt with' not only the Jews but whomsoever else they fancied.

It was quite a pleasant country, easy for driving as there were so few cars, but the sight of the areas which had been the ghettos in the towns was horrifying, and one wondered which people in Lithuania, or their parents or grandparents, had been parties to the slaughter and if they had changed.

The final major stop was in Vilnius, the capital. It was quite a pleasant city, we stayed at a comfortable hotel, and it all seemed very civilized. Then we were advised to visit Ponar Airfield. We drove there – we were the only visitors – and came across a horror-story of horror-stories. As we arrived we saw a goods train coming in, with wooden closed trucks, the sort of truck in which prisoners had been taken to the concentration camps. Then we found the history of Ponar: Before World War II there was the Molotoff-Ribbentrop Pact between Russia and Germany, where they drew a line as to the frontier and agreed that one would not trouble the other.

In the meantime the Russians decided to build an airfield there, and for fuel storage they dug eight very large craters into which they intended to put the fuel storage tanks. But before they could get as far as that the Germans invaded.

The Germans did not need another airfield but what were they to do with eight large craters? They had their answer: Fill them with dead Jews. They put Jews round the edge and machine-gunned them so they fell in, or threw them in and then shot them – or, even worse, threw them in and left them to die with more bodies, dead or alive, falling on them - until the craters were full. They then covered the whole lot with soil and turf. They were killing not only local Jews, but goods trucks similar to the one we had seen on arrival at Ponar that day were bringing Jews from other concentration camps where the gas chambers could not cope with the numbers.

In 1943 the Germans realised that there was a possibility that they could lose the War and so they decided to destroy the evidence: They got a thousand Jews and sent them down to dig up the covering earth and to put incendiary material among the bodies, and then gave them material to set it all alight – but at the same time pulled up the ladders. The result was, of course, that apart from destroying the evidence they killed the thousand Jews who had been working on the pits. Six of the eight pits today have been grassed over with some stone memorials, tasteful and sad but no more. But the Lithuanians had left two of the craters as they were, stark rock and deep and wide. It was difficult to hold back the tears, as indeed it is now even when I write about it.

The time came to leave Lithuania and we left, of course, from the same 'international' airport where we had arrived a few days before but now we had a little more time to look round – not that we needed any time as there was just one duty-free shop and one snack-bar. For all its faults I prefer Heathrow.

Being retired and taking advantage of it we had another cruise that year, again on Minerva, and this was to the Far East. We started at Singapore where we had been before but it will always carry a repeat, if only for the spotlessly clean loos. The first port of call was Bandar Seri Begawan in Brunei, the site of a most magnificent mosque, and then a cruise on a local boat along the waterways of Kampong Ayer. That consisted of a whole village, and quite a large one, built entirely on water, every building standing on stilts. We went, by invitation, into one house where they had drinks and snacks for us, but seeing a village like that really makes one appreciate the glories of Liverpool. The Sultan's Palace, and he is said to be one of the richest people in the world, looked, in the distance, to be quite fabulous. I say, 'in the distance', because it was well guarded and we could not get near.

I will not detail the various other stops save to say that it is a fascinating part of the world to visit. It included the Philippines with its markets, pottery makers, bicycle rickshaws, and a degree of poverty as bad overall as we had seen anywhere but at the same time with most excellent and imaginative museums, stone works of art and street monuments. But the people, the Filipinos, are so warm and friendly as they are all over to world, and one can understand why they will travel anywhere to make a living and, no doubt, to go somewhere a bit more financially attractive than their home country to enable them to send some money to their families.

The final leg was to Hong Kong. Minerva was a small ship, of some 12,000 tonnes. As we were preparing for bed we noticed sea-sick bags on every rail – indeed wherever they could be put. We soon found out why. We hit a monsoon, and by that I mean a monsoon. Minerva was tossed about like a cork. During the night Sonia got up to get a glass of water, and as she crossed, or tried to cross, the cabin Minerva was thrown about as if she were a paper bag blowing in the wind. Sonia was thrown down and hit the back of her head on a chair leg. There was blood all over the place and I immediately telephoned the ship's doctor, who was in our cabin, with a nurse, in minutes. We went down to his surgery where he put in five stitches to her scalp and then we were able to put her to bed. She was extraordinarily brave and uncomplaining, but then that is typical Sonia. The next day she got up and dressed when the monsoon subsided and apart from wearing a hat to cover the patch where the doctor had shaved and stitched, she carried on as normal. I shall never know how she does it.

In the meantime I was determined to have breakfast the next morning, and managed, by holding on to the rails on both sides, to get to the restaurant. The trouble was that when I got to the door there was a distance of about ten feet to get to a table. I had to wait to choose a moment – and I mean a moment - when the ship was comparatively steady and then dashed across to a table and sat down. I had to ask a waiter to get my breakfast from the various counters – breakfast was self-service - as I could not manage to stand, let alone move. I had a good breakfast but getting back to the cabin was difficult in that I had to get from the table to the corridor but fortunately I managed that, so far as I recall, without help. The great thing was that neither of us was sea-sick, and if we were not sea-sick then, we should never be sea-sick at all. This was in fact Minerva's last cruise before being taken out of service.

I must mention one cruise on Minerva at a later date, when the same ship was brought back into service. We went up for lunch and joined another couple at a table. I was next to the man and Sonia next to the wife. In the course of conversation, and they were very easy people with whom to converse, I mentioned that I had been articled – trained as a solicitor – in Birkenhead, which was on the Cheshire and North Wales Circuit. This chap mentioned that he had been a barrister practising on that circuit, and we exchanged names of people we remembered, those who were good and those who were not so good, those who had failed and those who had become judges, and so on. I told them that there was one chap I knew, a barrister, who was particularly good and a really delightful personality, and I said that his name was Emlyn Hooson. The man on my left almost jumped out of his chair, turned to me, and said "I'm Emlyn Hooson!". I turned him round full face, and indeed it was! I had not seen him for some fifty years but it was the same Emlyn. He went on from those times to take silk – to become a Q.C. - and had been Liberal Member of Parliament for Montgomeryshire until 1970 when he lost his seat, and had been sent to the House of Lords, being now Lord Hooson of Montgomeryshire.

He, and his wife – and she was the daughter of a knight as we discovered later – were the most unassuming and warm lovely people you could hope to meet. So many men in his position would have become such snobs. We have, I am delighted to say, kept in touch.

Anyway I must continue with the story: When we got back there was still plenty to do. Sonia gave a talk to the Jewish Historical Society on the Passover and she was elected President of the Liverpool Jewish Medical Society. Her great triumph was the final formal dinner when she secured, as the After Dinner speaker at the Annual Dinner, Professor Jonathan Halevy, the Director of the Shaare Zedek Hospital in Jerusalem, one of the largest hospitals in the capital. His talk was fascinating, particularly when he described the way in which Arab and Jew are treated equally and together. He told of one case where one of the nurses from the hospital was shot at by a terrorist on her way to work. Fortunately he missed. Soldiers nearby, however, managed to wound the assailant and took him to hospital – the Shaare Zedek! The Jewish woman he tried to kill was one of his nurses.

In January 2004 we had a cruise on Minerva II, a much larger ship of some 30,000 tonnes and some six hundred passengers, and it was indeed very comfortable. The old Minerva had been taken out of service but fortunately she is back again now. We started off at New Orleans which to me, as a jazz lover, would always be something very special. We saw among some other things the above-ground cemetery. As New Orleans is so low-lying, they cannot bury underground because a soon as they dug they would hit water. One interesting cemetery was the Jewish one, as Jews must be buried under the soil. So they have taken a large area as the cemetery and covered it with six or seven feet of soil, so that when somebody is to be buried they can dig down without hitting water!

The other part of the cemetery is all at ground level, with no 'soil build-up'. The 'final resting places' ranged from a hole in the front wall of a small stone building for poorer people to some very handsome monuments. Apparently with the 'hole-in-the-wall' ones they push the coffin and body into its slot. It is hot in New Orleans and the contents disintegrate pretty quickly, and so when the next one comes for burial they push in the new coffin, which in its turn pushes against the remnants of the previous one, which by now has disintegrated, and those remains fall at the back, further to disintegrate, so that the same slot can be used time and again. The wealthier ones had their own family 'graves', being more substantial buildings where there could be several members of the family, and places were usually left for those to arrive later.

The cruise took us along the coast south of the Gulf of Mexico to see the most remarkable Mayan remains. One thing that I had always queried with Mayan remains and particularly their pyramids was why the steps to the top were so large – some seventeen inches. I enquired and the answer was that with steps of that size you cannot walk down forwards, but have to walk backwards, so you never have your back to the gods.

We were given a chance to visit Honduras, which had until comparatively recently been a British colony, and ultimately arrived at the Panama Canal. That really was an experience, and going from east to west took the whole day, leaving only a few feet of clearance on either side. It would have been an amazing feat of engineering today, and so it is even more remarkable that they did it then. Never a dull moment.

Another good cruise in Minerva II was in the summer of 2005 where we visited, among other places, the Dardanelles and the battle-fields of Gallipoli. I am still stunned by the fact that Winston Churchill, the then First Lord of the Admiralty, could even have considered a landing here, but he was responsible for it. The British and the ANZACS (Australian and New Zealand Army Corps) landed on the narrow beaches, the Turks, who in the First World War were our enemies, were on the sharply rising hilltops, and it is amazing that the Allies managed to land at all. In fact they battled on for some six months and then had to give up, having suffered 250,000 casualties – for nothing. To read of it is one thing but to see it is another. We visited the Turkish trenches on the top of the hills, and looked down on the beaches where the Brits and ANZAKS had landed, and our hearts are still broken by such a traumatic experience. We stood, as well, on the beaches where the British and ANZAKS had been and found that experience even more traumatic.

-oOo-

Chapter 19
Jerusalem The Gold

We think cruising is worthwhile so long as the places we go to are worthwhile. Indeed we try to take a yearly cruise on Minerva with the great attraction of no dancing girls and no casino, but wonderful lecturers and very interesting ports of call. But one of our main 'holiday' destinations was and is Jerusalem, where our granddaughter Inbal, who married at eighteen, gave birth when she was nineteen, in March 2006, to a boy whom they have called Nevo. In May 2009 she gave birth to a daughter – ten pounds and no stitches! – called Noa Nina, the Nina being Hebrew for great-granddaughter, and it was also my Mother's name. Having our daughter, Nadine, three grandchildren and, at that time, one great-grand-child there, we clearly wanted to see quite a lot of the family and so instead of renting flats at inordinate rentals as we had done thitherto, we decided to buy a flat of our own. Nadine in fact found a flat for us to look at – we had seen many but none was really what we wanted – and this was situated in what is known as – although we did not know this at the time – the Cultural Mile. I have no idea why it should have that title as in Israel they work in kilometres, but the culture aspect was absolutely right. It was a flat within four minutes' walk of the Jerusalem Theatre, with its two large concert halls, a cinema, two theatres, a restaurant, a display area and a bookshop, and was also within easy walking distance of other cultural venues where there are regular lectures in English as well as in Hebrew, and a lot of the Hebrew ones have simultaneous translations into English. In addition on a Monday afternoon there is a free concert in the Jerusalem Theatre from five until seven pm, free because it is being broadcast and the noise of an audience makes it more interesting for the listener.

We looked at the flat and it seemed most suitable, and we wanted a one-bedroom flat to save us the embarrassment of people, including family, wanting to stay with us. We are not inhospitable but when you are away you prefer – or at least we prefer – not to have to use our energies looking after guests, however nice they may be. The flat was basically fine, and we managed to find a very good contractor who did all we asked to make the place like new. We had to go to buy furniture, light fittings and, indeed, everything that one has to do when buying a new property. It turned out to be excellent in every respect and staying there for weeks at a time was not only full of interest but, at that time, cheaper than living in England.

A couple of years later, having seen so many older people with Filipinos who help them in the house and to get about, we realised that one day we may need similar services, and we would need space for a Filipino to sleep. So in 2008 we changed flats. The new one is only a couple of hundred yards away from the old one, is on the third floor – with a lift, I hasten to mention – and wonderful views, not to mention the most superb sunsets. Someone had bought it to renovate it, and we got there in time to influence the renovations, and so it really is 'state of the art' with central air conditioning/heating, ultra modern, and with every comfort. It has three bedrooms, and we use one as a dressing room and one as a study, but were conversion required it would be no problem.

What we do as a rule when in Jerusalem is to go to what is known as an 'Ulpan', modern Hebrew language classes, two or three mornings a week. Sonia is, of course, in the top class and I am still struggling and gradually climbing up the ladder. Lectures, concerts and films and plays, cafes and restaurants and particularly the family, leave us with very little spare time. We have been lucky enough, too, by virtue of the efforts of a very lovely friend, Ra'anana Meridor, a retired Professor of Classics and whose son, Dan Meridor, has been a government minister for many years, and another son, Salai, has been the Israel Ambassador to the United States, to have a wonderful circle of friends. She used to invite us to her flat to meet people of interest – professors, judges, ambassadors and so on – and then when we bought our own flat she gave us their telephone numbers and then, on her advice, we invited these people to our home, they invited us back, and so the circle grows.

The saga continues and, so long as we are together, we hope that it continues for a long time to come. Retirement has tremendous advantages and I feel that there should be legislation to enable people to retire at, say the age of thirty-five, and then start work at sixty. Surely it is better to be younger and fitter to enjoy yourself than when you are at retirement age. I have suggested this to legislators but they take no notice – they may feel different when they are older.

One of the basic ingredients of having 'the good life' is to do the jobs you prefer to do and be with people you want to be with. My time as a solicitor, a judge and as a politician and local government leader were fascinating – serious enough if you did not take them too seriously. Sonia enjoyed her medical practice and continued to do locums for some years after she retired. But the main thing is to have a partner for life with whom you enjoy every moment. We, Sonia and I, may take it to the extreme in that even if one of us wants to post a letter the other will go with, but that is how we both tick and that is how we still feel about each other.

Sonia has been, and I hope will continue to be for years and years, a most wonderful wife in every possible respect. She is extremely learned and bright, and yet completely without conceit. Everything she does in the house, from cooking and entertaining to doing the laundry is without fault – except that I think that she is too modest. If you listen to a piece of music she will tell you not only the composer but his dates and probably when he composed it as well. She is a most competent public speaker – in fact anything you can mention, she can do, and do it well. I was the luckiest man in the world to have met her, and I congratulate myself every day on my having the intelligence to propose to her before anybody else could get in. And she is not holding a pistol to my head as I write this!

When I say 'Life is too serious to be taken seriously', I mean that. Plenty of things are sent to try us, and one can either cry or laugh, make the worst of it or the best of it. But there is nearly always a lighter side and that should always be fostered.

I wish all of you, who have managed to read all this, a life which you do not take too seriously, with somebody who takes only one thing seriously – you – and that you have a profession or occupation which you enjoy and which fills you with interest. And if something annoys you, you always have a choice – to laugh or to cry, and the former is surely preferable.

--oOo-

Epilogue

Having read through this book I suddenly realised the tremendous changes which have taken place in my lifetime, and I just wish to list a few of them. You, of any age, can no doubt do the same, but I think that the changes in my lifetime are far greater than at any other time in history – nothing to do with me! The future may, of course, show even more rapid changes.

For example, when we were young we visited Warsaw by boat and train and it took a week. Now it will take about three hours. Radios were crystal sets – we had a long aerial the length of the garden when I was a child, and the reception was there if you were lucky. Gramophone records were easily-breakable plastic and the sound would be completely unacceptable today. A symphony had to be recorded on to two sides of each of four or five records.

There was, of course, no television in my younger days. This came after the War. I clearly recall watching the Coronation in 1953, with about eight others, on a 9" or 12" screen – I forget which – in fuzzy black and white and all of us being amazed at the miracle. We could never imagine the present-day 42", or larger, flat colour screen, which itself will no doubt soon be out of date.

Hot water for the bath was from a fire or stove in the kitchen – it seems that the immersion heater had not been invented. We bought a one kilowatt heater for the hall when we first married which we hoped would heat the whole house. It probably made no difference other than psychologically. Anyway it was all we could afford. Even had we been able to afford it there was hardly any central heating in private houses unless they were stately homes.

When I was a boy, or indeed even when I reached manhood, no watches or clocks were controlled from the atomic clock – if you were within five minutes of the right time you were lucky. Of course you had to wind up your wristlet watch before going to bed every night – there were no battery-driven clocks or watches. There were no computers when I was first in practice – indeed I was one of the first solicitors to have a photo-copier, where I had to run off a copy of a document, rather like a negative before you get the photo, and then make a copy of the copy. I was one of the first solicitors to have FAX, but in those days – the 1980s, not so long ago - to send a sheet took about four minutes. One sheet!

I know I am jumping about the place, but the computer I am using to write this book was unheard of not so long ago. My typewriters had red and black ribbons, and if you made a mistake you had to rub it out on the letter and on the carbon copy or start again. I was one of the first solicitors to have a computer in the office, in the 1980s. We had six people dictating and six typing. When the letter was ready I could read it on my screen and correct it if necessary, and then press a button to print it. But the letters were gold-coloured on dark brown, which they said was easier on the eyes. The computer was the size of an old-fashioned filing cabinet and it had a hard drive of – wait for it – two hundred megabytes! - not enough for a child's toy these days.

I remember in 1938 my parents buying a 'fridge, and people came to look at it as it was so unusual. The flat iron was heated over the kitchen fire – electric irons had not been invented, or, if they had, they were used only by very special people.

When I was a child my mother used to telephone her parents in London. She would put in the call at about six in the evening and the operator said she would connect and ring back when the connection was made – about two hours later.

When we built our house in 1949 the heating was by a coke combustion stove which, when lit, heated the kitchen and gave us hot water. Our 'fridge had a capacity of one and a half cubic feet – most people did not have one at all – and it was cooled by gas heating!

Microwaves had not been not invented, nor were domestic dishwashers.

When a shirt was dirty – and one wore it for more than a day or two – it had to go to the laundry for washing. I, and most other people wearing a tie, and most people did, wore separate collars. I had stiff ones, which I wore for two or three days and then took them to 'Collars Ltd' to have them cleaned and starched.

Being cold in winter most men, including me, wore 'long Johns', long underpants down to the ankle, and a waistcoat was a must because otherwise it was too cold. Telephone connections, while I think of it, were mechanical: I went once to the main Liverpool telephone exchange, and saw these massive machines turning and going up and down as numbers were dialled. Today it is all a tiny fraction of the size and so much quicker because it is all done electronically like one great big computer. My first 'mobile 'phone', and that was in the car, involved an installation of the machinery under the whole of the back seat, an aerial from the roof of the car, and a handset on a wire next to me. It even worked most times!

Trains were steam and so journey times were twice those of today – in Japan with the Bullet Train they run about four times faster than in those days. Traffic lights did not exist. There were policemen on 'point duty' at most junctions. There were no traffic indicators – if you wanted to turn right you opened the window, however cold it was, and put your arm out. To turn left you did the same thing but waved your arm round and round. To show those behind that you were slowing down you put your hand out of the window and waved it up and down.

I remember a friend of my parents, Jack Brazil, visiting us and being very proud of his zip-fastener fly. We had never seen one before: It had only been buttons. Jack went to the loo but failed to return, and when my father checked it turned out that the zip had failed. Jack Brazil continued that day with safety pins.

A year or two before World War II the Sir Alan Cobham Air Display took place in Hull, and my father and I went there. Dad treated us both to a flight on an 8-seater de Havilland Rapide. We were amazed at the size and speed – and my father was terrified! We flew at a height of 1000 feet, imagine that, and at a speed of eighty miles per hour.

Cars had no heaters other than – if you paid quite a lot for it – a fan inside which recirculated the warm air. There as no change of air. The windscreen misted up unless you bought a little heater held on by rubber suckers, which sent a little hot air up the windscreen. The side and rear windows misted up. There were no wing- or door-mirrors, nor was there any anti-freeze.

Domestic tumble dryers had not been invented, and so there was only the 'wringer' to dry the clothes which were then hung up on a line in the kitchen, and the kitchen smells followed them to the drawer where they were kept.

You could never have thought of opening a car door without putting the key in the lock, or of opening the boot whilst still some way away – or indeed power steering, which we now take entirely for granted. You could not turn the wheel when the car was stationary, it was too stiff, and so you had to be moving backward or forwards to carry out your manoeuvre.

In those days one had to use money or write out a cheque – there were no credit cards.

I could go on indefinitely – but then so can you. Whatever your age, the changes in your lifetime are beyond belief, and will get faster and faster. I can only hope that methods of killing people, such as the atomic bomb, will not be as successful as those inventions which are sent to help us.

But there was another side. In my earlier days one could leave suitcases on the rack on top of the car, or in the open boot at the back, completely exposed, and they would not be stolen. There was no mass of traffic on the roads. Children respected their parents, in contrast to today when the children are in charge. Gun crime was almost unheard-of and 'binge drinking' had not even been invented.

The world has changed so much, but the question is as to whether or not it has changed for the better.

You just have to look round you to enable you to write your own list. The changes occur daily, there is always something new and your own equipment is always out-of-date. I would love to have a chance to have a look in, say, fifty years' time, but the chances of that are small!

-oOo-

Lightning Source UK Ltd.
Milton Keynes UK
31 July 2010

157625UK00001B/60/P